POLICY TRANSFORMATION IN CANADA

Is the Past Prologue?

Canada's centennial anniversary in 1967 coincided with a period of transformative public policymaking. This period saw the establishment of the modern welfare state, as well as significant growth in the area of cultural diversity, including multiculturalism and bilingualism. Meanwhile, the rising commitment to the protection of individual and collective rights was captured in the project of a "just society."

Tracing the past, present, and future of Canadian policymaking, *Policy Transformation in Canada* examines the country's current and most critical challenges: the renewal of the federation, managing diversity, Canada's relations with Indigenous peoples, the environment, intergenerational equity, global economic integration, and Canada's role in the world. Scrutinizing various public policy issues through the prism of Canada's sesquicentennial, the contributors consider the transformation of policy and present an accessible portrait of how the Canadian view of policymaking has been reshaped, and where it may be heading in the next fifty years.

CAROLYN HUGHES TUOHY is a professor emeritus of political science and founding fellow in public policy at the Munk School of Global Affairs and Public Policy at the University of Toronto.

SOPHIE BORWEIN is a PhD candidate in political science at the University of Toronto.

PETER JOHN LOEWEN is a professor of political science, global affairs, and public policy at the University of Toronto.

ANDREW POTTER is an associate professor at the McGill Institute for the Study of Canada.

Policy Transformation in Canada

Is the Past Prologue?

Edited by
CAROLYN HUGHES TUOHY, SOPHIE
BORWEIN, PETER JOHN LOEWEN,
AND ANDREW POTTER

UNIVERSITY OF TORONTO PRESS
Toronto Buffalo London

ISBN 978-1-4875-0430-4 (cloth)   ISBN 978-1-4875-2324-4 (paper)

Library and Archives Canada Cataloguing in Publication

Title: Policy transformation in Canada : is the past prologue? / edited
by Carolyn Hughes Tuohy, Sophie Borwein, Peter John Loewen, and
Andrew Potter.
Names: Tuohy, Carolyn Hughes, 1945- editor. | Borwein, Sophie, 1989-
editor. | Loewen, Peter John, 1979- editor. | Potter, Andrew, editor.
Description: Includes bibliographical references.
Identifiers: Canadiana 20190057440 | ISBN 9781487523244 (softcover) |
ISBN 9781487504304 (hardcover)
Subjects: LCSH: Policy sciences – Canada. | LCSH: Political planning –
Canada. | LCSH: Canada – Politics and government.
Classification: LCC JL86.P64 P65 2019 | DDC 320.60971 – dc23

University of Toronto Press acknowledges the financial assistance to its
publishing program of the Canada Council for the Arts and the Ontario
Arts Council, an agency of the Government of Ontario.

 Canada Council   Conseil des Arts
for the Arts   du Canada

 ONTARIO ARTS COUNCIL
CONSEIL DES ARTS DE L'ONTARIO
an Ontario government agency
un organisme du gouvernement de l'Ontario

Funded by the   Financé par le
Government   gouvernement
of Canada   du Canada

 Canadä

Contents

Part Three: Rethinking Sovereignty, Allegiance, and Rights

Part Four: Canada's Borders and Beyond

Preface

As significant anniversaries are wont to do, Canada's sesquicentenary inspired a number of projects of stock-taking and forecasting along the country's evolutionary path. This volume is the product of one such project. In November 2017, members of the Canadian policy community gathered at a two-day conference at the University of Toronto to reflect on public policymaking in Canada – to look both back at what the country has accomplished in the fifty years since its centennial, and forward at what it can hope to achieve in the decades to come. The conference was guided by an appreciation of the legacy of the burst of policymaking that characterized the centennial era, and by recognition of the magnitude of the country's contemporary challenges. It was animated by the idea that the challenges facing Canada today require a rethinking of public policy akin to what occurred five decades earlier, but tailored to the country's current demographic, economic, and social realities. How do the policy paths established in the centennial era, and shaped over subsequent decades, position us to address neglected and emerging policy problems? Which policies need to be built upon, which discarded, and which created anew?

This volume presents the policy agenda that emerged from this conference. It opens with an assessment of Canada's experience with innovative public policymaking in the last fifty years. In each of the following sections, policy experts address a core challenge for Canadian policymaking. Although the conference sessions from which these papers are drawn were organized around specific areas of public policy, certain themes emerged across sessions. This volume is organized to reflect these unanticipated but serendipitous synergies. Part One explores the different experiences and outlooks of successive generational cohorts as they confronted questions of investing for the future. Part Two recognizes the inextricable interconnections across issues of economic development and growth, environmental impacts and federalism in Canada's regionalized economy. Part Three shows how, perhaps unexpectedly, debates over "reasonable accommodation," environmental protection, and reconciliation between Indigenous and non-Indigenous peoples might intersect to drive a fundamental rethinking of concepts of rights and sovereignty that seemed much clearer in the mid-twentieth century. Finally, Part Four explores Canada's role as one nation among many in a world in flux.

Key insights from these chapters offer both hope and cause for concern. Canada has harnessed technological innovation throughout its history, and must prepare itself to benefit from the next disruptive wave that is both inexorable and imminent. Rethinking relations between Indigenous and non-Indigenous peoples could introduce greater diversity into Canada's foundational principles and common myths, and thereby provide a new understanding of sovereignty better suited to the twenty-first century. The country's relative success in managing substantial flows of immigration is one of its greatest strengths, but that openness, premised on relatively orderly and easily-managed migration such as refugee resettlement and highly-skilled economic immigration, may be strained as migrant flows become more chaotic (as in the case of asylum claimants). Canada's highly decentralized federation is under-appreciated as an effective institutional framework for marrying localized and pan-Canadian objectives, but the resilience of existing federal arrangements will be tested in at least two ways. First, unless fundamental systemic pressures in the healthcare system are addressed, a resumption of rising costs will strain provincial budgets. Second, the unevenly-distributed costs across regions of transitioning away from fossil fuels will make intergovernmental cooperation in addressing climate change increasingly unlikely. Perhaps most significantly, the large millennial generation that will have to wrestle with these issues must do so without many of the advantages enjoyed by their baby-boomer predecessors. Given these challenges, the book concludes by assessing Canada's scope for policy transformation in the next fifty years.

This publication is the culmination of more than a year's worth of effort, and would not have been possible without the partnership of the University of Toronto's School of Public Policy and Governance (now the Munk School of Global Affairs and Public Policy), the McGill Institute for the Study of Canada, the University of Calgary's School of Public Policy, the University of Laval's Centre D'analyse des Politiques Publiques, the Institute for Research on Public Policy, and Massey College at the University of Toronto. Stella Kyriakakis, Christina McIntyre, and Sean Willett's assistance was invaluable in planning the event, as was Christopher LaRoche's editing support in helping pull together this volume. Financial support was also generously provided by the Social Sciences and Humanities Research Council of Canada (SSHRC) and TD Bank.

POLICY TRANSFORMATION IN CANADA

Is the Past Prologue?

1 Downstream from the Centennial: Navigating Fifty Years of Policy Change

SOPHIE BORWEIN AND CAROLYN HUGHES TUOHY

Canada's 1967 centennial anniversary coincided with a period of substantive policy change in the country, when defining features of today's public policy landscape emerged. Central pillars of the modern welfare state were established; the federation was reenergized in a project of "cooperative federalism" and province-building; the accommodation of diversity was pursued through the institutionalization of bilingualism and multiculturalism; and the rights-oriented venture that would culminate in the adoption of the *Charter of Rights and Freedoms* was seeded.

The considerable policy achievements of the period deserve praise, but they should not distract from what was left unaccomplished. Despite the triumphs of the welfare state in the era, children coming of age today experience higher income inequality than did their parents raised in the centennial period.[1] Reconciliation between Canadian and Indigenous peoples remains elusive, a half-century after rights and freedoms emerged so powerfully on to the policy agenda. Human destruction of the environment, highlighted in Rachel Carson's 1962 book *Silent Spring*, persists as an intractable policy challenge.

Evidently, the challenges facing Canada at its sesquicentennial anniversary are substantial. Their solutions will require rethinking the country's social and economic policy frames, and a willingness among federal, provincial, municipal, and Indigenous governments to adapt. This chapter looks at the legacy of the last fifty years of Canadian policymaking and considers whether, institutionally and politically, Canada is fit to address the policy challenges it faces in the next fifty years.

Policymaking at Canada's Centennial

Canada at its centennial was undertaking largescale public policy change that would fundamentally reshape the country's policy landscape. Key foundations of the Canadian welfare state were realized. The Canada Pension Plan, Canada's contributions-based retirement income program, emerged in 1965 out of federal-provincial negotiations to address rising poverty rates among Canada's elderly population. A year later, Canada's national medicare system was expanded to extend universal health insurance beyond hospital care to include physician services. Also in 1966, the Canada Assistance Plan (CAP) – one predecessor of today's Canada Social Transfer – laid the foundations for federal government cost-sharing of social assistance with the provinces. The Canadian Student Loans Program, another innovation of the federal government during this period, was established to supplement the resources available to students requiring financial assistance to attend postsecondary education. In constructing and financing these programs, the federal government assumed a larger role than it had previously in safeguarding the social and economic well-being of Canadians.

It was also in the Canadian centennial era that policymaking contended seriously with diversity in the country, embedding diversity and multiculturalism within Canada's collective imagination. The Royal Commission on Bilingualism and Biculturalism's work over the decade led to the 1969 Official Languages Act, cementing French and English as the official languages of Canada, and the 1971 Multiculturalism Act, officially recognizing Canada as a multicultural society. Changes made to Canada's immigration system under the 1967 Immigration Act, while less symbolic, were arguably of even greater significance in engendering Canadians' general acceptance of diversity. The act facilitated non-European immigration by removing country-of-origin restrictions, while implementing a points system for economic immigration that favoured immigrants with strong employment and integration prospects – those with English or French proficiency, higher levels of education, work experience, and arranged employment in Canada. The consequent relative economic success of Canadian immigrants is often credited with sustaining support for immigration and tempering the xenophobic debates that have emerged elsewhere.[2]

Canadian policymaking in the 1960s suggested an outward looking country, eager to engage with the world. The country took its cues from the 1948 *Universal Declaration of Human Rights* and international civil rights movements in enacting the 1960 Bill of Rights, recognizing the fundamental freedoms and equal rights of Canadians. The Bill of Rights gave way to the 1982 *Charter of Rights and Freedoms* that today, alongside multiculturalism, has achieved an almost mythical status in the country. These emergent civil rights discourses also positively focused attention on the socioeconomic disadvantage of Indigenous peoples in Canada, but the result was a misguided policy of assimilation proposed in the Liberal government's 1969 White Paper.

The country tackled a number of issues that extended beyond its borders in the centennial period. Following then-Secretary of State for External Affairs Lester B. Pearson's role in the Suez Crisis, for which he won the 1957 Nobel Peace Prize, Canada increasingly defined itself as a nation of peacekeepers. The publication of Rachel Carson's *Silent Spring* in 1962 triggered sustained environmental awareness and activism internationally that was mirrored in Canada, setting in motion decades of changes to legislation affecting air, land, and water.

Although the 1960s were a watershed moment for Canadian policy-making, many of the policies that defined this period of transformative change had been several decades in the making. In some cases the policies of the 1960s built on previous policy experiments, while in other cases they were new responses to shifting societal and demographic realities. In the welfare state realm, many of the programs that emerged in the 1960s can be traced directly or indirectly to earlier innovations. The origins of the Canada Pension Plan can be found in the 1927 Old Age Pension Act that provided basic pension support to low-income seniors, based on the premise that the federal government had a responsibility to ensure Canadians had sufficient income in retirement. The extension of universal health insurance to physician services was similarly the result of the federal government's earlier success with the 1957 Hospital Insurance and Diagnostic Services Act, which publicly insured hospital care. These early welfare state programs, alongside other programs such as the 1940 Unemployment Insurance Act, laid both institutional and political foundations for the burst of social policymaking in the 1960s. Institutionally, a period of "province-building" engendered an openness to "cooperative federalism" in both federal and provincial governments. Politically, the federal Liberal Party had a strong partisan imperative to embrace an ambitious social policy agenda as essential to its own rebuilding after successive electoral defeats. The negotiations that developed in these circumstances provided the foundations for the broad federal-provincial social policymaking architecture that would continue through various permutations in the coming decades.

Other policy changes in the centennial era were catalyzed by social and demographic change. Canada's 1960 Bill of Rights was a response to gradually rising doubt about the adequacy of the government's protection of rights and freedoms following a series of domestic and international failures – the brutalities of Nazi Germany, the struggles to end racial segregation in the United States, and Canada's own treatment of Japanese-Canadians during the Second World War. At the same time, a newly assertive and nationalistic Quebec, undergoing rapid urbanization and industrialization from the 1940s onwards, was the impetus for the Royal Commission on Bilingualism and Biculturalism. The Commission's work in turn highlighted the cultural contributions of ethnic minorities in Canada at a time when the country witnessed a rapid expansion of its non-British and French ethnic population, welcoming from the 1950s onward large numbers of Eastern and Southern European immigrants, and subsequently non-Europeans.

As the 1960s came to a close, increasingly fervent Quebec nationalism, growing Indigenous activism in response to the 1969 White Paper, and louder demands for accommodation of diversity would drive policymaking for several more decades. This era of policymaking would hit a crescendo in 1982 with patriation, the entrenchment of a bill of rights in the constitution, and constitutional recognition of Aboriginal rights.

But by the mid-1990s, federal government enthusiasm for largescale policy change appeared to be waning. After two failed attempts at constitutional change with the 1987 Meech Lake Accord and the 1992 Charlottetown Accord, constitutional exhaustion had set in.[3] The share of government spending in the economy reached a peak in 1992 and, with some cyclical fluctuation following the business cycle, declined thereafter. With only modest differences in timing, governments at both federal and provincial levels focused on deficit reduction from 1993–1997, with dramatic effects on program spending. Real per capita spending on healthcare, as an example, declined by approximately 8 per cent from 1992 to 1996.[4] At the federal level, a newly elected Liberal government under Jean Chrétien launched a sweeping program review in 1994 aimed at reducing program expenditures. As part of this agenda, federal transfers to the provinces became less conditional and less generous. Finance Minister Paul Martin's 1995 "austerity budget" reduced federal transfers for healthcare, social assistance, and postsecondary education, merging them into a single integrated Canada Health and Social Transfer (CHST). In the process, all conditions on provincial social assistance programs, with the exception that provinces not impose residency requirements, were abolished. Canada's newly named "Employment Insurance" program emerged out of reforms to unemployment insurance that restricted eligibility and reduced benefits. The result was a marked reduction in the gains in income redistribution that had been made in the 1960s and thereafter.[5] Canada's tax-and-transfer system was a leader among OECD countries in redistribution from the mid-1980s to mid-1990s, but in the mid-1990s fell to the bottom of the group, where it stayed for the next decade.[6]

With the return of government books to balance at both federal and provincial levels in the late 1990s, a modest reinvestment in program expenditures began. In the realm of social policy, these new investments were focused almost entirely on healthcare, where spending rebounded sharply. (Social spending on programs other than healthcare decreased as a proportion of total government spending in Canada from the mid-1990s to the mid-2000s, while rising on average in other OECD nations.)[7] Federal reinvestment in healthcare came with a return to some degree of conditionality, but the new conditions applied only to targeted sinking funds directed at certain priorities such as primary care, while the underlying transfer continued to be conditional only on compliance with the provisions of the Canada Health Act. Meanwhile, with some variation across provinces and again allowing for cyclical fluctuations,[8] total government expenditure as a proportion of GDP returned to early 1970s levels, still well below its peak in the late 1980s and early 1990s.

The spending constraint of the 1990s left its legacy in the form of reduced government policy development capacity. Action taken by Stephen Harper's Conservative governments after 2006 added further constraints. The reduction of the Goods and Services Tax (GST) by 2 per cent shrank the government's fiscal footprint, and the cancellation of the long-form census deprived policymakers of the data needed to effectively micro-target social interventions. On the intergovernmental plane, the Harper government's preference for watertight federal and provincial jurisdictions underlay its commitment to reining in the use of the federal "spending power" (the convention that enables Ottawa to spend in areas outside of its jurisdiction), and to limiting other intrusions into areas of provincial authority. This approach was most notably on display when, following the expiration of the 2004 Health Accord in 2014, the Harper government acted unilaterally to reduce the generosity of the escalator for the federal transfer while also abjuring the sorts of targeted funding that had characterized the Chrétien-Martin Accords. The Justin Trudeau government, for its part, would subsequently maintain the reduced level of the escalator while also negotiating targeted transfers with each province.

A Return to the 1960s?

Canada's sesquicentennial gives us reason to look back to the country's last milestone anniversary. In retrospect, the 1960s can be seen as a time of policy innovation and change, driven by an audacious vision for a country coming of age. What could not be foreseen at that time was how soon economic shocks and cultural shifts would overtake that vision, dissipating the momentum that might have carried through to other areas of policy such as climate change and relations with Indigenous peoples.

The Canada that celebrated its 150th anniversary in 2017 is different in important ways from the country it was at its centennial. Canadian demographics have changed – the population is now older, more multicultural, and more urban. The provinces have emerged as mature actors in the federation. Globalization has brought intensified economic integration, a new geopolitical power map, and changing mindsets of multi-layered citizenship. The labour market has witnessed expanded rates of female participation, but also a diminishing of medium-skilled jobs, and an increase in part-time and other precarious work. Climate change is now at the top of the policy agenda for the Canadian government, as too is reconciliation and a renewed nation-to-nation relationship between Canadian and Indigenous peoples.

As we tackle these challenges, it is worth reflecting on what has worked best in the last fifty years of policymaking. We contend that the most important development of the period has been the emergence and entrenchment of a mature and resilient set of federal arrangements that have quietly defined Canadian policymaking from the 1960s to the current era. The contentiousness that characterized federal-provincial relations for much of that period should not blind us to the merits, real and potential, of the institutions of Canadian federalism themselves.

As Kevin Milligan shows in this volume, Canada over the last fifty years has developed a uniquely decentralized fiscal federation. Today, the country is an international outlier in subnational spending in that the largest bulk of spending occurs at the provincial, not national, level. Even excluding transfers from Ottawa, combined provincial and local own-source revenues today well exceed those of the federal government. This is a substantial change when compared to the half-century earlier, when subnational revenues constituted little more than half of the revenue of the federal government.[9]

Canada's federal and provincial governments have negotiated – or perhaps more accurately, stumbled into – arrangements that for the most part achieve a delicate balance between the federal government using its larger revenue base to ensure a comparable standard of living for all Canadians, and the provinces having greater capacity to tailor programs to the specific needs of their populations. To take one important example, the country has negotiated an efficient set of arrangements for socialized health insurance. Through a combination of per-capita federal transfers and general equalization grants, provincial governments can effectively draw upon a nationwide risk pool for a substantial portion of expenditure while retaining responsibility for program delivery. A necessary corollary is that we tolerate cross-provincial variation in the redistributiveness of public policy.[10]

While the provinces have come to control the largest share of government spending, the federal government has by no means been emaciated. When economic necessity has required it, the provincial governments have welcomed significant federal presence in areas within their jurisdictions – in handing responsibility for unemployment insurance to the federal government in 1940 and in establishing joint responsibility for pensions in 1965, for example.[11] The federal government has also commonly used its spending power to directly target policy interventions to sub-provincial constituencies. Examples include the 1998 Canada Millennium Scholarship Foundation that directed money to postsecondary education, the federal Gas Tax Fund to transfer federal gas tax revenues to the municipalities, and the Harper government's universal child care benefit to help fund parents' childcare costs.[12] These interventions have been contentious but accepted, in no small part because of another unusual Canadian innovation of the late 1950s and early 1960s – the ability of provinces to "opt" out of national programs while receiving federal compensation. Later entrenched in the 1982 Constitution Act, this power has enabled provinces, most notably Quebec, to retain the control they seek over their social programs.

Canada's persistence at its 150th anniversary, despite the ever-present challenges of regional alienation and Quebec secession, gives us reason to be optimistic about the resilience of our federal institutions. This resilience matters because policy responses to the country's major challenges in the next fifty years will depend, in no small part, on the adaptability of Canada's federal structures. While federal debt is projected to be sustainable over the next fifty years, the country's aging population will place increasing pressure on provincial debt via rapidly rising health expenditures. A rethink of how responsibility for taxation and expenditures is divided among jurisdictions will likely be required.[13] Climate change will also test the mettle of Canada's federation. As Kathryn Harrison argues in this volume, the Trudeau government's early success in garnering provincial support for a national carbon pricing plan has given way to interprovincial disagreement that will likely intensify as emission reduction targets become more ambitious, since the costs of adjustment will disproportionately burden resource-rich provinces. At the same time, the dynamics between federal, provincial, and municipal levels will increasingly be tested as Canadian cities assert themselves globally, but with inadequate funding and a constitutional dependence on the provinces. And all of these arrangements will be complicated if, in addressing Canadian injustices toward Indigenous peoples, the federal government honours its commitment to recognize Indigenous governments as a third-order of government.

Conclusion

Transformative change requires institutional capacity and political will. These conditions have existed in Canada before: the traumas of economic depression and war led to the cresting in the 1960s of an optimistic project of social renewal. Can we find analogous conditions as Canada enters the last half of its second century as a nation? Canada's challenges now are different. To some extent they represent the contemporary manifestations of problems not adequately addressed in the 1960s – most notably those relating to Indigenous peoples. Others represent newer phenomena – the pace of technological change and the rise in income and wealth inequality after the mid-1990s. But it may be that these very challenges are creating the conditions for transformative policy change. Institutionally, the need to build a new relationship between Indigenous and non-Indigenous Canadians is giving rise to new ways of thinking about sovereignty that have the potential to transform Canadian federalism, as Jean Leclair argues elsewhere in this volume. As for political will, the confluence of issues of Indigenous relations, environmental protection, migration, and economic change may drive the formation of new coalitions of interest, new political alignments, and new partisan agendas. In 2019, for the first time since the late 1970s, the baby boomers will no longer be the largest generational demographic in the Canadian electorate – they will cede that status to millennials.[14] Just possibly, the ground for transformative politics is being prepared.

NOTES

1 Miles Corak, "'Inequality is the root of social evil,' or Maybe Not? Two Stories about Inequality and Public Policy," *Canadian Public Policy* 42, no. 4 (November 2016): 367–414.

2 Keith G. Banting, "Is There a Progressive's Dilemma in Canada? Immigration, Multiculturalism and the Welfare State: Presidential Address to the Canadian Political Science Association, Montreal, June 2, 2010," *Canadian Journal of Political Science* 43, no. 4 (December 2010): 797–820.

3 Peter H. Russell, *Constitutional Odyssey: Can Canadians Become a Sovereign People?* (Toronto: University of Toronto Press, 2004).

4 Carolyn Hughes Tuohy, *Remaking Policy: Scale, Pace, and Political Strategy in Health Care Reform* (Toronto: University of Toronto Press, 2018), 378.

5 David Alan Green, W. Craig Riddell, and France St-Hilaire, *Income Inequality: The Canadian Story* (Montreal: Institute for Research on Public Policy, 2016).

6 Keith Banting and John Myles, "Introduction: Inequality and the Fading of Redistributive Politics," in *Inequality and the Fading of Redistributive Politics*, ed. Keith Banting and John Myles (Vancouver: UBC Press, 2013), 1.

7 Carolyn Hughes Tuohy, "Health Care Policy after Universality: Canada in Comparative Perspective," in *Inequality and the Fading of Redistributive Politics*, ed. Keith Banting and John Myles (Vancouver: UBC Press, 2013).

8 Most notably during and after the 2008 global recession.

9 Stephen Brooks, *Canadian Democracy* (Oxford: Oxford University Press, 2015), 252.

10 Rodney Haddow, "Labour Market Income Transfers and Redistribution: National Themes and Provincial Variations," in *Inequality and the Fading of Redistributive Politics*, ed. Keith Banting and John Myles (Vancouver: UBC Press, 2013), 381–409; Andrew Sharpe and Evan Capeluck, *The Impact of*

Redistribution on Income Inequality in Canada and the Provinces, 1981–2010 (Ottawa: Centre for the Study of Living Standards, 2012).

11 Kevin Milligan, "Canada's Radical Fiscal Federation: The Next Fifty Years," this volume.

12 Karine Richer, *The Federal Spending Power* (Ottawa: Library of Parliament, 2007).

13 Kevin Milligan, "Canada's Radical Fiscal Federation."

14 Edward Greenspon and Paul Adams, "Singh, Trudeau and the Triumph of the Millennial Voter," *IPolitics*, October 3, 2017, https://ipolitics. ca/2017/10/03/singh-trudeau-and-the-triumph-of-the-millennial-voter/; David Coletto, "The Numbers Don't Lie. The Conservatives Have a Millennial Problem They Have to Deal With," *Abacus Data*, May 27, 2017, http://abacusdata.ca/the-numbers-dont-lie-the-conservatives-have-a-millennial-problem-they-have-to-deal-with/.

PART ONE

Generational Prospects, Then and Now

2 Dreams along a Journey

MICHAEL VALPY

Judy LaMarsh, of all people, personified Canada on the 100th anniversary of Confederation. On the lip of the Sixties' sexual revolution, the fractious, ornery Liberal MP from Niagara Falls became only the second woman appointed to a federal cabinet (making no secret of her dislike for the Prime Minister, Lester B. Pearson, who appointed her). At the dawn of new symbols cementing Canadians' attachment to their country, she began the process, as Minister of National Health and Welfare, of shaping public medicare into law. As minister responsible for the centennial celebrations, she stood waist-deep in Yukon snow with the sleeves of a borrowed parka dangling below her fingertips and yodelled – she'd been practising – at members of the Yukon Alpine Club's centennial project as they set off to climb ten hitherto unclimbed peaks along the territory's border with Alaska and name them for the provinces.

She makes the national journey from centennial to sesquicentennial that much more interesting – and puzzling. The nation in 2017 would be almost unrecognizable to the nation of 1967, which most Canadians are likely okay with. But what turned off the 1967 sunshine? Where has the wish for transformative policies gone? Why is it that no one, nothing, speaks mythologically to us in the 150th year of Canada's official existence beyond, maybe, the tubby Canada C3 icebreaker that sailed from Toronto to Victoria? Is it true that we no longer have time for, or interest in, or the capability of, a unified vision, time for dreams, for national homophily, for a public life in common – or is it that those things never did exist outside a limited collection of our imaginations or actually still exist but are buried under fallen leaves? Whatever. The magic has gone missing ... and there is no new Judy LaMarsh.

In 1967, Canada was a country whose inhabitants fell in love with themselves and thrilled to the secret mysteries of their land. Journalist Bruce Hutchison, English Canada's mythologizer-in-chief, had written only a few years before: "All about us lies Canada, forever untouched, unknown, beyond our grasp.... My country is hidden in the dark and teeming brain of youth upon the eve of its manhood. My country has not found itself nor felt its power nor learned its true place. It is all visions and doubts and hopes and dreams."[1] Heady, lovely stuff.

Culture, demographics, and follow-the-leader primarily shape policies.

English Canada was just awakening from its decades' long sleep as a dozy, affluent, smug, delusionarily homogeneous, still proud with its wartime bravery, conservative, provincial society, largely unconcerned about poverty, about Indigenous people, about racism, and about the place of women beyond the kitchen and maternity ward. It was a place, in *Globe* columnist Doug Saunders's description, whose somnolent streets you'd have to leave if you wanted to make something of yourself (which can be still pretty much the case today).

Centennial interviews with provincial premiers, published in *The Globe and Mail* in 1967, showed their interests for the next half-century to be fixed on the banalities of harvesting more resource wealth with the concomitant rewards of job creation and investor profits – excepting Ontario's John Robarts, who was concerned about how Canada would absorb population growth, and Nova Scotia's Robert Stanfield, who hoped for a better partnership between anglophone and francophone Canadians. Jean Lesage of Quebec wanted a republic.

Quebec was substantially further down the road to being woke, to use a contemporary meme. By 1967, it was well through the door of the Quiet Revolution, rudely challenging anglophone and foreign business elites ("Our people are the waterboys of their own country," wrote poet Felix Leclerc, who was listened to), an ultra-conservative, autocratic church, a largely moribund public service and civil society, and Canadians in ROC who insisted on seeing the province as *comme les autres*.

Indeed, what passed uncommented-upon by the premiers – outside Quebec – were the Sixties' great tectonic shifts in Canadian society. The shifts of Quebec, women, the baby-boomer young, all ubiquitously touched by a prolonged, affluent, and tenacious Keynesian consensus.

Christian churches in French and English Canada emptied, a walkout led largely by young women who saw in the church a residual patriarchy they no longer wished to tolerate (Pope Paul VI's 1968 encyclical

Humanae Vitae banning artificial birth control was so resolutely rejected in Canada that even the country's Catholic bishops, in their Winnipeg Statement, distanced themselves from it). Within a decade premarital virginity was demoted from the centre of mainstream morality to the margins of conservative religious and ethnic groups. Women students in universities across Canada openly defied the Criminal Code prohibition against disseminating birth control information until the law was changed in 1969. Two years earlier, Pearson's Minister of Justice, Pierre Trudeau, had famously declared the state to have no place in the bedrooms of the nation and that "what's done in private between adults doesn't concern the Criminal Code." In centennial year, Trudeau legalized contraception, liberalized divorce laws, and decriminalized homosexuality. In the same year, Pearson created the Royal Commission on the Status of Women to ensure equality for women and report on issues regarding equal pay, child care, birth control, and women's education. In the mid-1950s – a mere 10 years before the 1967 centennial – only 23 per cent of women age 25 to 44, prime childrearing age, worked outside the home. By the mid-1960s, the figure was one-third and by the mid-1970s, it was nearly half. As the first wave of baby boomers left university in 1971, more than a third of the total labour force was female.[2]

And the young. It wasn't so much their numbers as it was their proportion of the population that gave them such impact on Canadian society. Their demographic bulge fixed the country's median age at 26 (whereas today, despite the presence of an almost equally large but proportionally smaller young generation – the millennials – the median age is 42).[3] The prospect of youthful restiveness made Pearson and his cabinet nervous. They looked at the rise of postwar social democracy in Europe. They looked across the border at the New Frontier – "the frontier of unfilled hopes and unfilled threats.... the frontier of uncharted areas of science and space, unsolved problems of peace and war, unconquered problems of ignorance and prejudice, unanswered questions of poverty and surplus."[4] They decided they must get in step.

Pearson was little interested in the centennial and he led a government that never achieved much popularity and still less excitement. But he did follow closely what was happening in the rest of the North Atlantic community, and beginning in the mid-1960s he and his government very much did assume a greater obligation to the Canadian populace which never received much applause, likely because it was expected. They created the Canada-Quebec Pension Plan, a new unemployment insurance plan, an equalization program for provinces less able to afford public services, public healthcare, a reduced threshold for Old Age Pension qualification, a guaranteed income supplement for the impoverished old, federal cost-sharing for a range of programs like childcare, assistance for postsecondary education and for people with disabilities, a flag, a Royal Commission on Bilingualism and Biculturalism, official language status for French, the U.S.-Canada Auto Pact (which opened the door to free trade in the auto industry), the world's first race-free – in theory – immigration policy, and a foreign policy that identified Canada with many former colonies emerging as independent nations.

The Pearson government also introduced a raft of programs offering young Canadians adventures in work, travel, and volunteer social services – which it did courageously in the face of often intense criticism from older Canadians, who saw the programs as a waste of taxpayers' money. It introduced a new era of cooperative federalism primarily aimed at Quebec. After a prolonged and politically clumsy debate, it refused to accept nuclear weapons on Canadian territory. Peacekeeping made Canada an exemplary citizen of the world.

Economic nationalism didn't take, a cross that Pearson's one-time Finance Minister and friend, Walter Gordon, carried with him into political banishment. Rachel Carson's *Silent Spring*, first published in 1962, caused a buzz of environmentalist talk but no government action.

Although Indigenous peoples' participation in the centennial was largely limited to feather headdress photo-ops, the government had commissioned UBC anthropologist Harry B. Hawthorn to investigate their socio-economic situation and his report, published in 1966 and little commented upon in the media, concluded they were the most marginalized and disadvantaged group in the country. Hawthorn labelled them "citizens minus," blaming years of bad government policy, especially the Indian residential school system that he recommended be shut down 20 years before it was.[5] The government responded with a White Paper proposing what was tantamount to – again – cultural assimilation, an idea it dropped in 1970.

The first bricks and mortar of multiculturalism were still in the distance. The country on its official 100th birthday was very white.[6] The population was 20.5 million. Today it is 35 million and very much not-so-white.[7] Yet we're still – as many young Canadians of colour are forcefully proclaiming – no more than paddling in multiculturalism's wading pool. Indeed, after 46 years of boasting that we're the best in the world at multiculturalism, we're still at multiculturalism 1.0.

There is a closetful of things to do, of issues to address, bucket lists of transformational policies that hold out promise for a smart journey into the next fifty years – and no national political party committed to a greater obligation to the Canadian populace. No sign, it seems, of anyone moving. One wonders when it was that we stopped asking ourselves who we are, stopped puzzling over what our identity is, stopped questioning what the bonds of our social cohesion are? Because that moment may have led us to stop dreaming about Canada as a better place.

The good news in 2017 is that EKOS Research Associates finds Canadians likely more attached to their country than are the inhabitants of any other Western nation. The uneasy news – it's not bad news yet – is that EKOS reports the importance of many longtime salient symbols of our nationhood is dramatically eroding. The significance of the beaver, the maple leaf, the flag, *O Canada*, hockey – yes, hockey – the Grey Cup, Parliament Hill, cultural diversity, tolerance, official bilingualism, Canada Day, Remembrance Day, and the RCMP have all declined.[8] This is glue becoming unstuck.

What do Canadians consistently tell pollsters they still value most about being Canadian? Medicare, now fifty years old and under stress. The *Charter of Rights and Freedoms*, now thirty-five years old. And Canada's national parks and a clean environment – the former 135 years old, dating back to the creation of Banff as the first national park, and linked often to the forced displacement of Indigenous and non-Indigenous residents within proposed park boundaries, and pressures for commercialization that have always been present. As for the environment, WWF-Canada reported in a June 2017 study that each of the country's twenty-five major watersheds faces multiple environmental threats, while the data needed to track changes and guide policymakers are either inaccessible or simply nonexistent.[9] And WWF-Canada's 2017 Living Planet Report found, after eighteen months of research, that half of all monitored vertebrate wildlife species in Canada (451 of 903) are in decline. And of those 451, the index shows an average decline of 83 per cent.[10] As settler colonialism destroyed Indigenous culture, it is now en route to destroying all life with which we share the land.

Multiculturalism is our biggest swagger but, for the first time since EKOS began asking the question in the 1990s, the number of Canadians who think the country is admitting too many immigrants who are people of colour has passed the 40 per cent mark – meaning we are not only souring on so many traditional national symbols but we also appear to be becoming more racist.[11] In fact, as we're discovering, Canada is a society of systemic racism which we are reluctant to discuss. For every dollar that white Canadians earn, Canadians of colour earn 81.4 cents and see themselves not fitting, not being the Canadian norm, branded officially by their national government with the demeaning labels of visible minorities and ethnic minorities even though in Canada's largest city – and soon to be other major cities – the visible minority is white. Indigenous people appeared only peripherally on the celebration agenda in 1967. In 2017, not a lot of them want to appear at all. Quebec's more than six million francophones have about as much attachment to the country as they do to their neighbour's cat, says EKOS president Frank Graves. But he adds: "I don't think that's necessarily a problem. I think what's been established is a new healthy détente where Quebeckers are able to pursue their own thing and there's a nice civic nationalism where we agree on things."[12] Not necessarily a problem *yet*, but an element – along with the sentiments of the Indigenous occupants of the land – that inevitably is going to lead us to the painful necessity of a reborn federalism. Canada, in political scientist Peter Russell's words, is a country of one multicultural lump and two never-finished conquests and that can't go on forever unchanged.

The sunshine of 1967 has gone behind the clouds of economic stagnation – the economy is moving forward but individuals aren't; so much of the gain is being appropriated by cadres at the top. It has gone behind the clouds of middle class decline. At the turn of the century, 70 per cent of Canadians told EKOS they were middle class; today only 45 per cent identify themselves that way while 38 per cent idcntify as working class, well above the historical norm of 20 per cent (the numbers are similar in the United States).[13] This self-identified working class in Canada are upset and angry and, some evidence suggests, beginning to gravitate toward the Conservative Party.[14] The concern is that these discouraged Canadians – following their sisters and brothers in the United States and United Kingdom – will come to be faces of rejection of elite authority, of rising right-wing or so-called ordered populism – what *The Economist* calls "drawbridge up populism" – and of authoritarianism.

The cause of intergenerational equity lies barely in the long grass. Canadians of all generations, but especially millennials, tell EKOS they are open to interventionist government – but how are governments responding? Canadians face a patchwork of provincial coverage on dental care and effective long-term care that is in large part inadequate to their needs. What will governments say to a generation that can't afford to live in the cities where they grew up? How will governments say they have met millennials' dreams about the environment when withdrawals from the resources' bank are still treated as if the account is bottomless? Are Canada's government and its opposition parties advocating a face for the country to the world of which the majority of its citizens can be proud, as they were in 1967?

"We are in the midst of a fourth industrial revolution, driven by disruptive technological change," Kevin Lynch, former Privy Council clerk and now BMO vice-chair, wrote in *The Globe and Mail* six months ago.

> These technologies, such as big data, machine learning, artificial intelligence, quantum computing, and blockchain are intersecting and combining in extraordinary ways to create a "technology 4.0 world." Few revolutions unfold without upheaval, uncertainty and swaths of winners and losers, however, and this one is no different. Its impact will be felt well beyond commerce in how we communicate, interact, date, learn, gather news, and govern ourselves.[15]

With it, says Lynch, is the quandary of "the growing gap between the scale, scope and speed of these transformations and the capacity of government to implement timely and effective policy changes. Put simply, in today's dynamic world, last-generation governance and policy processes are a poor match for next-generation disruptive trends, and trust in government is an early casualty."

A scary – but exciting – time to be Canadian.

NOTES

1 Bruce Hutchison, *The Unknown Country: Canada and Her People* (Westport, Conn.: Greenwood Press, 1977), 3.
2 Doug Owram, *Born at the Right Time: A History of the Baby-Boom Generation* (Toronto: University of Toronto Press, 1996), 276.
3 Frank Graves, "Canada 150: Our National Mood in Four Easy Charts," *Policy*, August 2007, 10.
4 John F. Kennedy, "Accepting the Democratic Party Nomination for the Presidency of the United States" (July 15, 1960), http://www.presidency.ucsb.edu/ws/index.php?pid=25966.
5 *Statement of the Government of Canada on Indian Policy* (Ottawa: Queen's Printer Cat. No. R32–2469, 1969).

 6 Peter S. Li, "Cultural Diversity in Canada: The Social Construction
    of Racial Differences," Strategic Issue Series (Department of Justice
    Canada, 2000), http://www.justice.gc.ca/eng/rp-pr/csj-sjc/jsp-sjp/
    rp02_8-dr02_8/rp02_8.pdf.
 7 Statistics Canada, "Immigration and Ethnocultural Diversity: Key Results
    from the 2016 Census," *The Daily*, October 25, 2017, https://www150.statcan.
    gc.ca/n1/daily-quotidien/171025/dq171025b-eng.htm.
 8 Frank Graves, "Broad Shifts in Public Outlook on Values, Identity, and
    Symbols" (May 16, 2017).
 9 WWF-Canada, "A National Assessment of Canada's Freshwater,"
    Watershed Reports (WWF, 2017), http://assets.wwf.ca/downloads/
    WWF_Watershed_Reports_Summit_FINAL_web.pdf?_ga=2.231352287.
    1761277905.1531778695-1994878753.1531778695.
10 Zoological Society of London and Environment and Climate Change
    Canada, "Living Planet Report Canada" (WWF, 2017), http://www.wwf.ca/
    newsroom/reports/lprc.cfm.
11 Graves, "Broad Shifts in Public Outlook on Values, Identity, and Symbols."
12 Michael Valpy, "Fifty Years after Lovefest '67 Witness the Rise of 'Sourpuss
    Nation': Valpy," *The Toronto Star*, June 27, 2017, https://www.thestar.com/
    opinion/commentary/2017/06/27/fifty-years-after-lovefest-67-witness-
    the-rise-of-sourpuss-nation-valpy.html. See also Stuart N. Soroka, Richard
    Johnston, and Keith Banting, "The Ties That Bind? Social Cohesion and
    Diversity in Canada," in *Belonging? Diversity, Recognition and Shared Cit-
    izenship in Canada*, ed. Keith Banting, Thomas J. Courchene, and F. Leslie
    Seidle, vol. III, The Art of the State (Montreal: Institute for Research on
    Public Policy, 2007), 561–6.
13 Frank Graves, "From the End of History to the End of Progress: The
    Shifting Meaning of the Middle Class" (August 19, 2014), http://www.
    ekospolitics.com/index.php/2014/08/from-the-end-of-history-
    to-the-end-of-progress/.
14 "Through a Lens Darkly: Shifting Public Outlook on the Economy and
    Social Class" (EKOS politics, October 10, 2017), http://www.ekospolitics.
    com/index.php/2017/10/through-a-lens-darkly/; "Political Landscape
    Deadlocked: Tax Proposals Not Hurting Government, May Well Help"
    (EKOS politics, October 3, 2017), http://www.ekospolitics.com/index.
    php/2017/10/political-landscape-deadlocked/.
15 Kevin Lynch, "How Disruptive Technologies Are Eroding Our Trust in
    Government," *The Globe and Mail*, May 1, 2017, https://www.theglobeandmail.
    com/opinion/how-disruptive-technologies-are-eroding-our-trust-in-
    government/article34857043/.

3 Discounting Now and Then

JOSEPH HEATH

Most major public policy initiatives have an impact on both social welfare and government finances, not just in the present, but extending out into the distant future. Since it is possible to distribute the benefits and burdens of these policies in different ways over time, such policies naturally raise questions of intergenerational justice. Unfortunately, the treatment of these questions has historically been somewhat ad hoc. This has been changing, driven in particular by the need to respond to the problem of anthropogenic climate change, an issue in which the distribution of burdens over time winds up being a significant determinant of policy choices. Perhaps the single most important factor determining this distribution is the social discount rate used in public sector cost-benefit analysis. The discount rate is used to calculate the present value of future costs and benefits, and as such literally determines how much we are obliged to care about the sorrows and triumphs of those yet unborn. The higher the discount rate, the lower the level of concern that must be shown, in the present, for future costs and benefits.

Despite its evident importance, the social discount rate for a long time languished in obscurity. Historically, it was determined in a rather casual manner and the rates tended to be quite high. In Canada, for instance, the social discount rate was fixed in 1976 at 10 per cent.[1] This was considered plausible in most of the standard cases of application, which typically involved infrastructure projects. The only anomaly was nuclear waste disposal, which is necessarily concerned with events in the very distant future. Such an anomaly was relatively easy to ignore, however, because it is practically impossible to construct any sort of model in which it matters at all in the present what happens 10,000 years from now. However, as the use of cost-benefit analysis expanded and became standard in more policy domains – such as environmental regulation and healthcare resource allocation – the choice of discount rate began to loom larger. The issue that most brought it to the fore-front, and into broader public consciousness, was climate change.

Climate change policy has a peculiar feature: because of "inertia" in the atmospheric system, the effects of any carbon abatement policies that we adopt now will only begin to be felt in approximately 50 years, and will peak in 80 to 100 years. The discount rate functions like the inverse of the interest rate – it is an exponential function – and as a result generates a phenomenon quite similar to the "miracle of compound interest." In the same way that retirement savings accumulate rather slowly on a timescale of 10 to 20 years, but then begin to take off as the compounding effect kicks in, the discount rate also tends to make little difference on a timescale of 10 to 20 years, after which the effects of compounding begin to accumulate. On a timescale of a century the effects are massive. Imagine, for instance, that some disaster was likely to occur that stood poised to destroy half of Canada's current agricul-tural output, a loss with a market value of over CDN $54 billion. If we anticipate that the event will occur in 100 years, a 10 per cent rate of discount suggests that we should be willing to spend no more than $1.436 million in the present to prevent this disaster from occurring. Should we elect not to, on the grounds that preventative action would have cost $1.5 million, it seems reasonably certain that our descendants would one day spit on our graves and curse our short-sightedness.

Because of this, climate change policy recommendations are ex-tremely sensitive to the discount rate employed to calculate the social cost of carbon (SCC). This was dramatized in 2006 with the release of the *Stern Review on the Economics of Climate Change* in the U.K., which recommended the immediate imposition of carbon taxes an order of magnitude larger than those being contemplated in mainstream policy circles.[2] Critics went through the 700-page report with a fine-toothed comb, trying to find the basis for this rather surprising conclusion. They found that Stern's assessment of the science, as well as the Integrated Assessment Model he used for projecting damages, were all unremark-able. The only real difference, it turned out, was that Stern rejected the mainstream view on social discounting, and instead chose to use a rate of only 1.4 per cent. As result, his model simply assigned much greater weight to damages occurring in the distant future, and therefore de-manded much greater sacrifice from present generations.

Stern's recommended carbon tax rates were not implemented in the United Kingdom or elsewhere, and the report remains an outlier in the more general debate over the SCC. It did accomplish two things, however, beyond merely drawing attention to the importance of the discount rate. First, it solidified support for a "normative" specification of the discount rate (based on the "Ramsey formula") in lieu of the economist's traditional preference for a "revealed" or "positive" basis for determination. Second, it contributed to a general trend that has seen discount rates being lowered in Europe and North America. Canada has been party to this trend, although not to the degree seen in many European countries.

On the first issue, the traditional approach to discounting was based on a calculation of the opportunity cost of state spending. The thought was that when a public investment is made, and the state raises tax revenue in order to fund it, this means that the resources are no longer available for private investment. Thus in order to produce a net benefit to society, the return on the public investment should be at least as large as that on the foregone private investment.[3] One way of ensuring this is to discount the benefits of the public investment at the prevailing rate of return on private investment (or "capital" more generally). The problem with this approach is that the rate of return on private investment reflects a number of worries that private individuals have, but which the state need not concern itself with. Most obviously, equity returns contain a "risk premium" that is inapplicable to state investments. As a result, where it was once common to look at the rate of return on equities when determining the discount rate, common wisdom now among those who recommend a "positive" approach is to look at the long-run rate of return on "risk-free" investment vehicles, such as U.S. Treasury Bonds.[4]

There is, however, another problem that arises: the rate at which individuals discount the future reflects their own fear of death, and thus individuals demand a relatively high rate of return before becoming willing to forego consumption. Public investments, by contrast, are made to benefit "citizens" abstractly, not any particular set of individuals, and thus the fact that some will die and others will be born is an irrelevant consideration. Yet because it is impossible to disentangle this "fear of death" factor from other elements in the individual's discount rate, there is no way to get an appropriate social discount rate by aggregating individual rates. Using the rate of return on capital is just an indirect way of getting at aggregate individual rates, since the relatively high marginal productivity of capital is a consequence of the relatively low willingness of individuals to save, in part because they fear death. As a result, many theorists – including, most prominently,

Kenneth Arrow – have argued that the social discount rate cannot be inferred from any set of empirical observations or measurable quantities; it must be determined normatively.[5]

The standard template for a normative specification of the discount rate is the "Ramsey formula," which incorporates three considerations: the first is the rate of growth of the economy multiplied by the "elasticity of marginal utility of consumption" which, taken together, represent the rate at which the marginal utility of consumption is expected to decline over time.[6] The thought here is simple: because we are concerned about utility and not resources *per se*, and we know that marginal utility declines as consumption levels increase, we can expect that if economic growth produces an increase in the overall consumption level over time, future generations will be less sensitive to costs and benefits. They will, in other words, not care as much about a particular cost or benefit if they are much richer than we are. And because they may not care as much, neither should we.

There is a common confusion on this point that should be avoided. The "elasticity of marginal utility of consumption" term – or *eta* – is often misrepresented as specifying a level of *inequality aversion*. This is not strictly speaking correct. Although it *could* be used to represent inequality aversion, in the standard Ramsey formula it is a "positive" measure, used only to represent the fact that marginal utility declines with increased consumption. This is necessary in order to make the formula welfarist, or utilitarian; it does not involve the introduction of any supplementary egalitarian or prioritarian commitments.

The final two considerations are introduced in a single term – usually *delta* – which represents the combination of risk (the probability that the outcome will not be realized), and a pure time preference (a simple preference for outcomes that can be achieved *sooner* over those that can be achieved *later*). The risk term is, of course, the one that looms large in individual discount rates because of fear of death, but in a social discount rate is either ignored or else set to a very low value to reflect the probability of human extinction. (If everyone dies in a nuclear holocaust, then we need not worry about climate change. It follows from this, however, that because there is some small probability each year of a nuclear holocaust, then we should be somewhat less worried about the effects of climate change the further removed these effects are from the present.)

So far these values can all be set empirically. It is the final term, the pure time preference, that is obviously normative and which, on the basis of moral arguments, many theorists are inclined to set at zero. (This is, for instance, what generated Stern's ultra-low discount rate.) These arguments are not uncontested. Theorists of a more consequentialist persuasion who are inclined to set it at zero usually do so on the grounds that "location in time," just like "location in space," is a morally irrelevant feature of events, and so the significance of harms cannot be discounted for proximity in either space or time.[7] This argument is problematic, however, because it leaves the theorist having to introduce empirical postulates in order to avoid infinite utility streams (since time extends out infinitely into the future). Theorists of a more egalitarian persuasion who are inclined to set the time preference at zero do so because they consider such a preference discriminatory, since it appears to treat people who are born later as worthy of less concern than those who are born earlier.[8] This is largely an illusion produced by poor framing of the problem, however. Discounting a utility stream treats everyone's welfare exactly the same *at the time that it is realized*. It is only when the welfare is in the future that it counts for less than welfare in the present. To put this point more technically, discounting does not reduce the value of future welfare, it only reduces the *present* value of future welfare. If the same discount rate is applied uniformly over time then everyone is treated equally because everyone's welfare is discounted by the same amount, at the same life stage.

These are somewhat philosophical considerations. The more influential arguments have been slightly more pragmatic ones, pointing out that while the ultra-low discount rates that result from setting the time preference to zero may produce intuitively satisfactory results in the domain of climate change, they are unreasonably, perhaps even absurdly, demanding when applied in other policy domains. When one considers what the rate of savings should be, for instance, or what the balance of investment should be in healthcare versus healthcare research, zero time preference suggests that present generations should be sacrificing almost everything in order to benefit individuals living in the distant future.[9] This helps to accentuate the strangeness of the view that prohibits us from showing any partiality toward the interest of real, flesh-and-blood human beings, existing in the present, because we could be showering much greater benefits upon people who will be born only after the passage of centuries.

The underlying concern is that analysts like Stern were gerrymandering the discount rate in order to support a set of policies that seemed intuitively appropriate to the case of climate change, but that could not be seriously contemplated in other domains. What Arrow recommended, by contrast, was essentially a "reflective equilibrium" procedure, working out first what seemed like reasonable policies in various domains, then determining the implicit discount rate. Unfortunately, finding a single rate that supports the full range of intuitively plausible policy judgments has proven elusive. Thus what theorists have been gravitating toward is a variable discount rate that declines over time for long-term investments.[10] There are various ways of motivating a declining rate, with perhaps the most straightforward being Martin Weitzman's suggestion that it is a consequence of uncertainty about the correct discount rate.[11] Again, because of the effects of compounding, in order to keep estimates of the value of a discounted utility stream within a fixed range of uncertainty, it is necessary to push down the discount rate as one goes further into the future. This approach is one that has been adopted by some governments, most notably the United Kingdom, which uses an official rate that begins at 3.5 per cent but then begins to decline over a 30-year horizon, eventually reaching 1 per cent for effects beyond the 300-year mark.

This arrangement strikes many as acceptable, although perhaps only as a kluge. To the extent that it generates dissatisfaction, it is because the changing rate has the potential to generate time-inconsistent policy recommendations. For instance, a policy that has effects over 100 years in the future might be cost-benefit justified, and thus adopted, but then become unjustified 25 years later, due to nothing other than the passage of time. In such cases, the state winds up confronting a problem that is strictly analogous to weakness of will in the individual, where one must find a way to pre-commit to policies in anticipation of one's own future preference reversals. This is, it should be noted, only a theoretical difficulty so far – one that is being carefully ignored in policy circles. It may someday become a practical difficulty as well.

Setting aside this issue, it remains the case that throughout the world states have been lowering their discount rates, and Canada, despite being something of a laggard, is not an exception. The United Kingdom lowered its official short-term discount rate from 6 per cent to 3.5 per cent with the publication of the *Green Book* in 2003. The European Union has had the unenviable task of having to harmonize social discount rates across member states, a process that has tended to push all countries in the direction of the state with the lowest rate, which is, unsurprisingly, Germany. In Canada, the rate of 10 per cent, adopted in 1976 and reaffirmed in 1998, was lowered in the 2007 Treasury Board

Canadian Cost-Benefit Analysis Guide to 8 per cent in standard cases.[12] This is still quite high, so in 2016 when the Ministry of Environment and Climate Change determined the SCC, it used a rate of 3 per cent (based on a rather loose interpretation of the Treasury Board guidance).[13] At the same time, economists have consistently pressured the Government of Canada to lower its overall rate and adopt a time-declining rate for longer-term projects. Since the 2007 guide was not particularly comprehensive, it would not be surprising to see official movement toward a lower rate in the near future.

NOTES

1 Treasury Board of Canada Secretariat, "Canadian Cost-Benefit Analysis Guide: Regulatory Proposals," 1976; Anthony E. Boardman, Mark A. Moore, and Aidan R. Vining, "The Social Discount Rate for Canada Based on Future Growth in Consumption," *Canadian Public Policy* 36, no. 3 (September 2010): 325–43.

2 Nicholas Stern, *The Economics of Climate Change: The Stern Review* (Cambridge, UK: Cambridge University Press, 2007); William Nordhaus, "Critical Assumptions in the Stern Review on Climate Change," *Science* 317, no. 5835 (July 2007): 201–2.

3 Christian Gollier, *Pricing the Planet's Future: The Economics of Discounting in an Uncertain World* (Princeton: Princeton University Press, 2013), 22.

4 Gollier, 25–7.

5 Kenneth J. Arrow, "Intergenerational Equity and the Rate of Discount in Long-Term Social Investment" (December 1995), http://www.mv.helsinki.fi/home/valsta/Arrow-97-005.pdf.

6 Kenneth J. Arrow, "Discounting and Public Investment Criteria," in *Production and Capital*, Collected Papers of Kenneth J. Arrow, v. 5 (Cambridge, Mass: Belknap Press, 1985), 223; Joseph Heath, "Climate Ethics: Justifying a Positive Social Time Preference," *Journal of Moral Philosophy* 14, no. 4 (August 14, 2017): 440.

7 Derek Parfit, "Energy Policy and the Further Future: The Social Discount Rate," in *Energy and the Future*, ed. Douglas MacLean and Peter G. Brown (Totowa, N.J.: Rowman and Littlefield, 1983), 31–7.

8 Simon Caney, "Climate Change and the Future: Discounting for Time, Wealth, and Risk," *Journal of Social Philosophy* 40, no. 2 (June 2009): 163–86.

9 Arrow, "Intergenerational Equity and the Rate of Discount in Long-Term Social Investment."

10 Kenneth Arrow, M. Cropper, C. Gollier, B. Groom, G. Heal, R. Newell, W. Nordhaus, R. Pindyck, W. Pizer, P. Portney, T. Sterner, R.S.J. Tol, and M. Weitzman, "Determining Benefits and Costs for Future Generations," *Science* 341, no. 6144 (July 26, 2013): 349–50.

11 Martin Weitzman, "Why the Far-Distant Future Should Be Discounted at Its Lowest Possible Rate," *Journal of Environmental Economics and Management* 36, no. 3 (1998): 201–8.

12 Treasury Board of Canada Secretariat, "Canadian Cost-Benefit Analysis Guide: Regulatory Proposals," 2007, https://www.tbs-sct.gc.ca/rtrap-parfa/analys/analys-eng.pdf.

13 Environment and Climate Change Canada, "Technical Update to Environment Canada's Social Cost of Carbon Estimates," March 2016, http://ec.gc.ca/cc/default.asp?lang=En&n=BE705779-1.

4 Postponed Adulthood, the Inequality Surge, and the Millennial Burden

JOHN MYLES

I come from the infamous generation that entered young adulthood in the 1960s. I was born in 1943 in the shadow of Auschwitz and Hiroshima. Ironically, that made me part of what is no doubt the "luckiest generation" of the twentieth century. In the postwar years my family was living through the greatest economic boom in human history. I graduated from high school in 1960, just in time to take advantage of the postwar expansion in university education. When we completed our degrees, jobs were plentiful and wages were rising. The 1960s were also a period of equality-enhancing policy reform, including national health insurance, expanded public pensions, unemployment benefits, and social assistance.

The millennial generation's transition to adulthood is very different. By the standards of my cohort, the traditional markers of moving into adulthood – leaving home, achieving financial independence, marriage, and parenthood – have all been postponed or delayed, with important economic and social implications. And the inequality surge of recent decades means millennials will constitute a more divided generation than mine. Many of them will have good lives but many others will be less lucky. Postponed adulthood began with the late boomers and for them it was something of a novelty; for millennials, it is the new normal.

I report on recent research suggesting that the generations, both young and old, have adapted to these circumstances, moving into what we might think of as a new equilibrium in the social and economic life course. But I conclude with a discussion of why we might want to worry about the "new normal." Demographers worry about the effects of postponed adulthood on fertility and population aging. The OECD worries about "squandering our investment" in the most educated generation in human history. I worry most about what one might call the millennial burden. Millennials are being called on not only to finance our old age but also to make huge investments in the environment, public transit, early childhood education, and all of the other good stuff my generation failed to do. I worry that the new normal will put a damper on their enthusiasm for these big projects.

The Evolution of Postponed Adulthood

There are two views of millennials, cohorts born since 1980. On the one hand, they come from smaller families and thus have had more parental attention and economic resources at their disposal. Since they have fewer siblings, they also have more family resources to share and their inheritances when their parents pass away will be proportionately greater. They are certainly more highly educated than any previous generation. Their lifestyles and consumption patterns reflect the incredible technological revolution of the past 30 years. Most significantly, young women have been the beneficiaries of the "gender revolution" in education and employment since the postwar decades. Most of the young women from my high school cohort moved quickly into marriage and motherhood. Women were still a rarity when I went to university in 1960 but now outnumber men in our postsecondary institutions.

The millennials' gains have come at a price, however. For my generation – the birth cohorts of high industrialism and today's retirees – the transition to adulthood occurred early in life. By the 1960s, young adults were leaving home, getting married, and having their first children much sooner than any of the cohorts that had preceded them.[1] Most of us were employed, married, and had our first children by our mid-twenties.

Since the late 1970s, all that has changed. Marriage and first childbirth now occur in the late twenties or early thirties, at just about the time that people are beginning to establish themselves in real career jobs. Marriage and fertility rates are down and large numbers of young adults are living with mom and dad into their twenties and thirties. Labour market indicators of later adulthood began to emerge around 1980, catching the late boomers as they entered their twenties. Male earnings data from this period demonstrate the trend.[2] From the late 60s until roughly 1981, real wages and salaries grew by approximately 20 per cent in all age groups. Thereafter, a clear age division emerged: wages continued growing for those over 45, flattened for those age 25 to 44, and declined for younger workers.

These wage trends, of course, only tell the boys' story and ignore the gender revolution – the dramatic rise in female educational attainment, labour force participation, and earnings levels among young women born after 1960. Bringing women into the narrative complicates the story but doesn't change the conclusions. The early and tight coupling of the major adult transitions of my generation peaked in the late 1970s.[3] Thereafter, the average ages of leaving home, first marriage, and parenthood all began rising and clustering in the late twenties or the early thirties for both men and women. This had both social and economic consequences. Clark shows that, on average, a 30-year-old in 2001 had made the same number of transitions as a 25-year-old in 1971. As he concludes, the transitions of today's young adults are both delayed and elongated.[4] Does all this matter?

Families' later start has resulted in a reduction in fertility, down to 1.5 births per woman in 2006 and the same number in 2016.[5] Young adults are far from realizing the OECD's surveyed ideal family size of 2.3 children, and this difference between their preferences and outcomes represents a real welfare gap. Fertility clinics are booming as a result. In economic terms, postponed adulthood means that both the cumulative earnings and the accumulated wealth of adults in their mid-thirties have fallen dramatically since the end of the 1970s. Morissette and Zhang show that by 2005, the median wealth of young families whose members are between ages 25 to 34 was down 50 per cent from 1984.[6]

Millennials: A Divided Generation

The growing economic divide between younger and older workers of the 1980s was a canary in the coalmine, alerting us to the broader surge in income inequality that became evident in Canada by the 2000s.[7] This growing economic divide is already evident among millennials and will continue to mark them as they move through into their forties. David Macdonald shows that a large and growing wealth gap is evident among families whose members are as young as 20 to 29.[8] In 1999, top decile families in this age group held 66 per cent of their cohort's wealth and had median wealth of CDN $280,000. By 2012, the top decile held 72 per cent of their cohort's wealth, with a median value of $540,000. Clearly some young adults are getting off to a very good start indeed.

Growing economic inequality has multiple sources rooted in labour markets, politics, and demography. While it remains unclear how the specific evolution of labour markets and politics will alter millennial futures, the *demographic* drivers of the growing divide in their generation are already in place.

The first demographic divide in the millennials' world of dual-earner families is between single adult households with little labour to sell and households with two or more adult earners. Declining marriage and high divorce rates, especially among the less educated, mean the number of vulnerable singles is rising. Single-earner households – with or without children – are at greater economic risk. Less than 10 per cent of Canadians in the bottom income quintile live with a partner. In the top quintile, the figure is 90 per cent.[9]

The second divide that will persist over the working lives of millennials has two sources: the division between the educationally advantaged and disadvantaged, and the multiplier effect of marital homogamy, the tendency of like to marry like. Morissette and Johnson show that between 1980 and 2000, couples where both partners had university degrees saw their average annual earnings rise between 14 and 22 per cent.[10] Couples where both partners had high school education or less had stagnant or declining earnings. Earnings homogamy, the correlation between husbands' and wives' earnings, has also risen.[11] In 1980 the association resembled an inverted U: in two-adult households with children, women married to men in the lower middle of the earnings distribution – earning CDN $30,000 to $40,000 annually – had the highest earnings, while women married to men with higher earnings were less likely to be employed. By 2000 all this had changed. In 2000, the relationship between husbands and wives earnings was monotonic: the highest paid women were married to the highest paid men and the lowest paid women to the lowest paid men.

A New Life Course Equilibrium?

For the late boomers and Generation X, postponed adulthood was something of a novelty. For millennials, it is the new normal. The early and tight coupling of adult transitions of my generation is ancient history and humans adapt. Not surprisingly, then, recent research indicates that generations, young and old, have adapted, moving into what we might think of as a new equilibrium in the social and economic life course. A major study of U.S. millennials by the PEW Research Center entitled *Confident, Connected and Open to Change* captures the tone of this research. PEW reports that nine in ten millennials say that they either currently have enough money or will eventually meet their long-term financial goals.[12]

I left home at 17 and find it difficult to imagine living with mom and dad into my late 20s. But according to Katherine Newman's rich comparative study of young adults living at home, only Japanese parents seem upset by the situation.[13] In Japan, 28-year-old Akiro anticipates that he may move out of his parents' home by the age of 35. Akiro's mom, like many Japanese parents, is deeply troubled by his failure to live up to the ideals of masculinity and adulthood that she considers normative. She believes that all this is her fault, however: Akiro's retreat from maturity is the product of her coddling and lack of toughness when he was younger.

By contrast, life is sweet for 30-year-old Giovanni in Italy. His biggest expenses are going out on weekends and holiday travel. As Giovanni reports, nobody is surprised that someone his age is living at home and no one is pressuring him to leave. Only one of mother Maria's three adult children has moved out, and she is quite content to have the other two at home as she moves into late middle age.

In the United States, Newman reports, father William is enjoying the company of son John again as John saves up to pursue a postgraduate degree. In the meantime, John is building his C.V. by volunteering for a three-week trip to Africa, financed by dad, to work in a mobile health clinic. Paradoxically, young Swedish adults who still leave home in their early 20s complain about the weak bonds between themselves and older generations.

Reading Newman's accounts made me wonder whether my concern for the next generation is simply a bad case of boomer nostalgia for the way things used to be. And as it turns out, things were only that way for a brief moment in time. The early transition to adulthood of my generation, not the late transitions of millennials, is the historical anomaly. U.S. data on men age 20 to 30 living at home between 1900 and 2000 show that living with mom and dad was much more common in the first half of the twentieth century than it is today.[14]

So Why Should We Worry?

Demographers worry about the effects of postponed adulthood on fertility and, by extension, population aging. The reason is that while the social and economic life course has changed, the biological life course has not.

The OECD worries about social and economic waste. A 2015 OECD report concludes that we are "squandering our investment" by producing a generation with high levels of education but no place to go. Skills and talents that go unused during periods of unemployment or employment in "junk jobs" tend to atrophy with time. The share of 15-year-olds in Canada with good test scores on the Programme for International Student Assessment (PISA), an international study of educational systems by the OECD, is well above the OECD average. But our 16 to 29-year-olds fare less well; the per cent with poor literacy and numeracy scores is above the OECD average.[15] The main reason usually offered for this sort of discrepancy is weak integration of our educational system with the labour market.

My main worry, however, is that millennials will be either unable or unwilling to invest in the future: to take up the huge financial and political burdens we are expecting them to carry as they move into their forties. The fact that they will be paying for aging boomers for the next 30 years is often raised but is only one of their challenges. Millennials will be the main revenue source for financing the future costs of saving us from global warming, solving our problems with public transit, providing investments in early childhood education, and all the other good things that need doing.

All of these projects require new investments and *patient* investors. By definition, *investment* requires foregoing current consumption in the short run to get returns in the long run. In many cases, the returns are unlikely to be realized for several decades. Advocates for more social investment in early childhood education make the case that it will produce a future generation of young adults better equipped to function in a knowledge-based economy. If we start investing heavily in two and three-year-olds tomorrow, however, it will take a quarter of a century before we can expect measurable changes in employment and wage outcomes for young adults.

The moral of the story is that my generation has not always set a good example for those who are following us and that probably counts as a serious case of intergenerational injustice. It remains to be seen whether a generation whose adulthood has been both delayed and divided will meet these challenges. I worry that postponed adulthood, a growing economic divide, slow economic growth, and an ethos of no new taxes will put a damper on their enthusiasm for these big projects.

NOTES

1 Roderic Beaujot, "Delayed Life Transitions: Trends and Implications," in *Canada's Changing Families: Implications for Individuals and Society*, ed. Kevin McQuillan and Zenaida R. Ravanera (Toronto: University of Toronto Press, 2006), 105–32.

2 René Morissette, John Myles, and Garnett Picot, "Earnings Polarization in Canada, 1969–91," in *Labour Market Polarization and Social Policy Reform*, ed. Keith G. Banting and Charles M. Beach (Kingston, ON: School of Policy Studies, Queen's University, 1995), 23–50.

3 Beaujot, "Delayed Life Transitions."

4 Warren Clark, "Delayed Transitions of Young Adults," *Canadian Social Trends* 84 (Winter 2007): 14–22.

5 Beaujot, "Delayed Life Transitions," 124; see also Statistics Canada, Table 13-10-0418-01: Crude birth rate, age-specific fertility rates and total fertility rate (live births), https://www150.statcan.gc.ca/t1/tbl1/en/tv.action?pid=1310041801.

6 René Morissette and Xuelin Zhang, "Perspectives on Labour and Income – Revisiting Wealth Inequality," *Perspectives on Labour and Income* 7, no. 12 (December 2006): 5–16.

7 Nicole Fortin, David A. Green, Thomas Lemieux, Kevin Milligan, and Craig W. Riddell, "Canadian Inequality: Recent Developments and Policy Options," *Canadian Public Policy* 38, no. 12 (June 2012): 121–45.

8 David Macdonald, "The Wealth Advantage: He Growing Wealth Gap Between Canada's Affluent and the Middle Class" (Vancouver: Canadian Centre for Policy Alternatives, June 25, 2015), https://www.policyalternatives.ca/wealth-advantage.

9 Special tabulation provided by Brian Murphy, Statistics Canada.

10 René Morissette and Anick Johnson, "Earnings of Couples with High and Low Levels of Education, 1980–2000," Analytical Studies Branch Research Paper Series (Statistics Canada, October 13, 2004), https://econpapers.repec.org/paper/stcstcp3e/2004230e.htm.

11 John Myles, "The Inequality Surge: Changes in the Family Life Course Are the Main Cause," *Inroads: A Journal of Opinion* 26 (Winter/Spring 2010): 66–73.

12 Pew Research Center, "Millennials: Confident. Connected. Open to Change," February 24, 2010, http://www.pewsocialtrends.org/2010/02/24/millennials-confident-connected-open-to-change/.

13 Katherine S. Newman, *The Accordion Family: Boomerang Kids, Anxious Parents, and the Private Toll of Global Competition* (Boston: Beacon Press, 2012).

14 Elizabeth Fussell and Frank F. Furstenberg Jr., "The Transition to Adult-hood in the Twentieth Century: Race, Nativity, and Gender," in *On the Frontier of Adulthood: Theory, Research, and Public Policy*, ed. Richard A. Settersten Jr., Frank F. Furstenberg Jr., and Rubén G. Rumbaut (Chicago: University of Chicago Press, 2005), 29–59.

15 Organisation for Economic Co-operation, *OECD Skills Outlook 2015: Youth, Skills and Employability* (Paris: OECD, 2015).

5 Half a Century of Pension Reform in Canada[1]

DANIEL BÉLAND

Public pension reform re-emerged as a key policy issue during the years leading up to the 2017 sesquicentennial anniversary of the Canadian confederation. This is the case in part because of the rise after the 2008 financial crisis of a political push to expand the Canada Pension Plan (CPP) and the Quebec Pension Plans (QPP), two closely-coordinated programs created in the mid-1960s, just before the country's centennial. In this short chapter I return to the initial debate leading to the advent of CPP and QPP, before turning to the recent debate about their expansion. Comparing and contrasting the debate over the creation of CPP and QPP in the mid-1960s with recent discussions over the expansion of these programs allows us to think about the future of public pension reform in Canada. Because of the multilayered nature of Canada's public pension system, we cannot study CPP and QPP in isolation from the evolution of other key components of this system. I start therefore by looking at the pension programs that existed in Canada before the mid-1960s.

Before the Centennial Era

The first national pension legislation in Canada was the 1927 Old Age Pensions Act (OAP), which provided a means-tested pension of CDN $20 per month to poor people age 70 and older who had resided in Canada for at least 20 years[2] The implementation of this legislation across the country required provincial participation, with provinces initially having to provide half of the funding. In 1931, to convince more provinces to participate in OAP, the federal government increased its contribution to 75 per cent. Quebec agreed to participate in OAP only in 1936, a decision that made OAP available in all provinces.[3]

In 1951, after constitutional negotiations with the provinces (necessary because pension reform fell under provincial jurisdiction), Parliament adopted Old Age Security (OAS). OAS was a purely federal program that eliminated the means-test associated with OAP to offer a flat pension to people age 70 and older who met residency criteria. Meanwhile, the Old Age Assistance Act (OAA) "extended means-tested benefits to those aged 65–69 and remained in place until 1970 by which time the age of eligibility for the universal pension (OAS) had been reduced to 65."[4] This new public pension system existed alongside voluntary occupational pensions and, after 1957, Registered Retirement Savings Plans (RRSPs), which were created to encourage people to save for retirement.

The Centennial Era

Despite the postwar growth in occupational pensions and the creation of RRSPs, it became increasingly clear to observers that Canada's modest public pension system centered on OAS could not guarantee the economic security of older people. Although the labour movement and the Cooperative Commonwealth Federation (CCF) pushed for meaningful pension reform in the mid-late 1950s, it was only in 1963, with the election of Lester B. Pearson's Liberal minority government, that this issue moved to the forefront of the federal policy process.[5] This stemmed in part from the progressive turn of the Liberal Party of Canada in the aftermath of the 1960 Kingston conference: there, the party adopted a more ambitious social policy agenda, with pension reform forming integral part.[6] Soon after the 1963 election, the Pearson government formulated a pension blueprint before discussing the creation of an earnings-related public pension program with the provinces (this later became the Canada Pension Plan).[7] A key turning point in these discussions came the following year when Quebec Premier Jean Lesage formulated the province's own pension proposal.[8] Lesage's belief in the need to create Quebec's own pension plan was rooted in part in his government's policy objective of depositing pension surpluses in the future *Caisse de dépôt et placement du Quebec*, a public investment board oriented toward investing in the province's economy as part of the push for French Canadian entrepreneurship, something that proved central to the Quiet Revolution. Lesage's proposal forced the Pearson government to revise its own proposal and expand the scope of the proposed CPP, which would exist alongside the nearly identical QPP.[9]

The creation of CPP and QPP in the centennial era represented a key turning point in the development of the Canadian public pension system. Offering a modest replacement rate of 25 per cent, the programs would complement both voluntary pensions and personal savings and also coexist with the OAS which, starting in 1967, became closely linked to the Guaranteed Income Supplement (GIS). Initially conceived as a temporary measure to help low-income seniors until the maturation of CPP and QPP, GIS is an income-tested program that soon became a permanent feature of Canada's public pension system. The very existence of GIS, which works in tandem with OAS, has meant that the system is more redistributive and more effective in fighting old-age poverty, which declined dramatically between the late 1960s and the late 1990s.[10]

The Legacy of the Centennial Era

In the field of pension reform, the centennial era was a major turning point. The creation of CPP, QPP, and GIS helped improve the economic security of older Canadians, making Canada a world leader in fighting elderly poverty.[11] At the same time, the centennial era also witnessed a rapid decline in fertility rates that marked the end of the postwar baby boom that peaked in 1959 with 3.94 children per woman. By 1972, the fertility rate had fallen below the reproduction rate (2.1), before declining even more after that.[12] In 2015, Canada had a fertility rate of 1.6, compared to about 2.5 in 1967.[13] The projected rise in the proportion of the population of persons over 65 years of age had a negative impact on the fiscal sustainability of CPP and QPP, which came under intense scrutiny in the mid-1990s. At that time, Ottawa and the provinces reached an agreement on CPP reform that led to significant changes to the program, including a gradual increase in the payroll tax from 5.6 to 9.9 per cent in 2003. Quebec enacted a similar reform to address the fiscal sustainability of QPP. In the end, CPP reform proved successful from both political and a fiscal standpoints because it moved the program back on a sustainable path. By increasing the contribution rate, the reform shifted CPP towards partial advance funding, thereby addressing concerns about intergenerational equity[14] The same cannot be said of the QPP reform, which failed to fix the long-term fiscal challenge facing the program, a situation related to Quebec's less advantageous demographics.[15] In 2011, the Quebec government decided to gradually increase the QPP contribution rate from 9.9 to 10.8 per cent, making it higher than the CPP rate for the first time since the creation of the programs in the mid-1960s.[16]

Although the changes to CPP and QPP enacted in the mid-1990s and (for QPP only) and 2011 have helped secure the long-term fiscal future of these two programs, the 2008 financial crisis helped create a new path for pension reform that fully materialized during Canada's sesquicentennial era. As opposed to events in the mid-1990s, this new push for pension reform involved an expansion of CPP and QPP benefits.

The Sesquicentennial Era

The 2008 financial crisis hit the pension savings of millions of Canadians while also drawing attention to the vulnerability of occupational retirement schemes, the gradual decline in their overall coverage, and their gradual shift from defined-benefit to defined-contribution pensions. These shifts have transferred demographic and economic risks from the employers operating these schemes to their workers.[17] Concerns about the adequacy of public pensions existed before 2008 but growing economic insecurity associated with the financial crisis and the recession that followed helped legitimize a push for an expansion of CPP and QPP benefits, whose modest replacement rates of 25 per cent had remained unchanged since the creation of both programs during the centennial era.[18]

Unsurprisingly, the New Democratic Party (NDP) and the Canadian Labour Congress led the charge on CPP expansion alongside left-leaning pension experts; the Canadian Labour Congress proposed a major increase in the payroll tax to finance an increase in the program's replacement rate from 25 to 50 per cent. In office since February 2006, Conservative Prime Minister Stephen Harper was not ideologically or politically predisposed to support an expansion of CPP benefits. Yet, because the Conservatives had a minority government, they did at least have to consider reform. To this end, Finance Minister Jim Flaherty held public consultations on CPP reform and then publicly supported the idea of a modest increase in CPP benefits in June 2010.[19] The small-business lobby and other elements of the Conservative base were strongly opposed to even this modest change, prompting Harper to explicitly abandon the idea later that year.[20]

Although the public campaign in favour of CPP expansion did not stop with the election of a Conservative majority government in May 2011, the concrete political opportunity for CPP reform re-emerged only after the victory of the Liberal Party in the October 2015 federal election. During the 2015 campaign, Liberal leader Justin Trudeau had embraced CPP expansion and, once in power, his government launched discussions with the provinces in an effort to bring about pension reform. Among the provinces, the Ontario Liberal government had been the most forceful in pushing for CPP expansion, threatening to create an Ontario Retirement Pension Plan if CPP benefits were not increased. The Quebec Liberal government, however, was not so keen on the idea of CPP expansion as it would have increased pressure within the Quebec political system to increase QPP benefits, a move the powerful provincial labour movement and some of its political allies had already embraced. It is important to highlight that Quebec's Liberal government, led by Premier Philippe Couillard, was more fiscally conservative than its Ontario counterpart under the leadership of Premier Kathleen Wynne. In June 2016, however, the federal government and eight of the provinces reached an agreement on CPP expansion (Quebec abstained and Manitoba signed later). As part of this agreement, the CPP replacement rate was set to rise from 25 to 33.3 per cent and the payroll tax rate from 9.9 to 11.9 per cent between 2019 and 2023. The maximum earnings limit will increase from $54,900 to $82,700 between 2016 and 2025.[21]

As anticipated, the expansion of CPP announced in June 2016 pressured the Couillard government to increase the QPP's replacement rate to mirror the CPP's rate. At first opposed to this idea, the Couillard government later accepted it.[22] In early November 2017, legislation was tabled in the National Assembly to expand QPP benefits along the lines of the CPP expansion announced the previous year.[23] Not expanding QPP benefits would have been politically risky for the Couillard government ahead of a provincial election set to take place in October 2018.

Because CPP and QPP expansion is fully funded, higher pensions should benefit primarily people who will reach age 65 several decades from now.[24] There is something remarkable about this expansion, which goes against the trend of most other advanced industrial countries, where pensions are trimmed rather than expanded.[25]

The Future of Public Pension Reform in Canada

The debate over CPP and QPP expansion during the sesquicentennial era should not obscure other looming issues related to the future of Canada's multilayered public pension system. First, OAS and GIS are financed out of the federal government's general revenues. In a context of accelerated population aging, rising pension costs are a significant issue for the federal treasury. Because the Trudeau government cancelled the decision to increase the eligibility age for both programs from age 65 to 67, as previously announced by the Harper government in 2012, other ways to mitigate the negative impact of population aging on the federal budget will have to be considered. This includes the extraction of new tax revenues.

Second, it is important to recognize the limits of occupation pensions and savings vehicles such as RRSPs in providing economic security to future waves of Canadian retirees. This is true in part because these voluntary schemes only cover a fraction of the working population. Considering this, further improvements to pension regulations and to the public pension system might be necessary in the future. The recently-announced increase in CPP benefits is not a silver bullet, especially if occupational pension coverage continues to decline over time.

Finally, while a lot of attention has been paid to OAS, CPP, and QPP in the sesquicentennial era, GIS remains a pivotal program in terms of fighting poverty among older people in Canada. Improvements to GIS benefits could help Canada further reduce poverty rates among vulnerable elderly populations, including Indigenous peoples, single women, and foreign-born citizens, all of whom are at high risk of falling into poverty.[26] While Canada has spent less public money on retirement security since the centennial era than many other advanced industrial countries, its public pension system has been remarkably successful in fighting elderly poverty and efforts to maintain and even improve.[27] Our record in this regard should extend beyond the sesquicentennial era.

NOTES

1 The author thanks Rachel Hatcher and John Myles for their comments and suggestions. He also acknowledges support from the Canada Research Chairs Program.

2 Kenneth Bryden, *Old Age Pensions and Policy-Making in Canada* (Montreal: McGill-Queen's University Press, 1974).

3 Keith G. Banting, "Canada: Nation-Building in a Federal Welfare State," in *Federalism and the Welfare State*, ed. Herbert Obinger, Stephan Leibfried, and Frank G. Castles (Cambridge, UK: Cambridge University Press, 2005), 89–137.

4 Daniel Béland and John Myles, "Stasis Amidst Change: Canadian Pension Reform in an Age of Retrenchment," in *Ageing and Pension Reform Around the World*, ed. Giuliano Bonoli and Toshimitsu Shinkawa (Cheltenham: Edward Elgar Publishing, 2005), 252–72.

5 Kristina Babich and Daniel Béland, "Policy Change and the Politics of Ideas: The Emergence of the Canada/Quebec Pensions Plans," *Canadian Review of Sociology* 46, no. 3 (August 2009): 253–71; Bryden, *Old Age Pensions*.

6 P.E. Bryden, *Planners and Politicians: Liberal Politics and Social Policy, 1957–1968* (Montreal: McGill-Queen's University Press, 1997).

7 Bryden, *Planners and Politicians*; Richard Simeon, *Federal-Provincial Diplomacy: The Making of Recent Policy in Canada* (Toronto: University of Toronto Press, 1972).

8 Dale C. Thomson, *Jean Lesage and the Quiet Revolution* (Toronto: Macmillan of Canada, 1984), 188.

9 Stephen Brooks and A. Brian Tanguay, "Quebec's Caisse de dépôt et placement: tool of nationalism?" *Canadian Public Administration* 28, no. 1 (March 1985): 99–119; Mario Pelletier, *La Machine à milliards: l'histoire de la Caisse de dépôt et placement du Québec* (Montréal: Éditions Québec/Amérique, 1989).

10 Béland and Myles, "Stasis Amidst Change"; Michael Wiseman and Martynas Yčas, "The Canadian Safety Net for the Elderly," *Social Security Bulletin* 68, no. 2 (February 2008): 53–67.

11 Wiseman and Yčas, "Canadian Safety Net."

12 Anne Milan, "Fertility: Fewer Children, Older Moms," *Statistics Canada*, November 13, 2014, http://www.statcan.gc.ca/pub/11-630-x/11-630-x2014002-eng.htm.

13 World Bank, "Fertility Rate, Total (Births per Woman): Canada," accessed April 10, 2018, https://data.worldbank.org/indicator/SP.DYN.TFRT.IN?locations=CA.

14 Alan Jacobs, *Governing for the Long Term: Democracy and the Politics of Investment* (Cambridge, UK: Cambridge University Press, 2011); Bruce Little, *Fixing the Future: How Canada's Usually Fractious Governments Worked Together to Rescue the Canada Pension Plan* (Toronto: University of Toronto Press, 2008).

15 Edward Tamagno, "A Tale of Two Pension Plans: The Differing Fortunes of the Canada and Quebec Pension Plans" (Ottawa: Caledon Institute of Social Policy, 2008), http://www.caledoninst.org/Publications/PDF/667ENG.pdf.

16 Daniel Béland and R. Kent Weaver, "Fork in the Road for Canada and Quebec Pension Plans," *Policy Options*, August 18, 2017, http://policyoptions.irpp.org/magazines/august-2017/fork-road-canada-quebec-pension-plans/.

17 Gerard W. Boychuk and Keith G. Banting, "The Canada Paradox: The Public-Private Divide in Health Insurance and Pensions," in *Public and Private*

Social Policy (London: Palgrave Macmillan, 2008), 92–122; Jacob S. Hacker, "Privatizing Risk without Privatizing the Welfare State: The Hidden Politics of Social Policy Retrenchment in the United States," *American Political Science Review* 98, no. 2 (May 2004): 243–60.

18 John Myles, "Income Security for Seniors: System Maintenance and Policy Drift," in *Inequality and the Fading of Redistributive Politics*, ed. Keith Banting and John Myles (Vancouver: UBC Press, 2013), 312–34. The "great pension debate" of the early 1980s witnessed an unsuccessful attempt to raise the CPP contribution rate; see Béland and Myles, "Stasis Amidst Change."

19 Bill Curry, "Flaherty Proposes Raising Canada Pension Payroll Premiums," *The Globe and Mail*, June 10, 2010, https://www.theglobeandmail.com/news/politics/flaherty-proposes-raising-canada-pension-payroll-premiums/article1599932/.

20 Daniel Béland, "The Politics of the Canada Pension Plan: Private Pensions and Federal-Provincial Parallelism," in *How Ottawa Spends, 2013–2014: The Harper Government: Mid-Term Blues and Long-Term Plans*, ed. Christopher Stoney and G. Bruce Doern (Montreal: McGill-Queen's University Press, 2013), 67–87.

21 Department of Finance Government of Canada, "Backgrounder: Canada Pension Plan (CPP) Enhancement," fact sheet, September 19, 2016, https://www.fin.gc.ca/n16/data/16-113_3-eng.asp.

22 Béland and Weaver, "Fork in the Road."

23 Angelica Montgomery, "Quebecers to Pay More, Get More from QPP, Starting in 2019," *CBC News*, November 2, 2017, http://www.cbc.ca/news/canada/montreal/pension-plan-enhancement-quebec-province-1.4384699.

24 Government of Canada, "Backgrounder."

25 John Myles and Paul Pierson, "The Comparative Political Economy of Pension Reform," in *The New Politics of the Welfare State*, ed. Paul Pierson (Oxford: Oxford University Press, 2001), 305–33.

26 Patrik Marier and Suzanne Skinner, "The Impact of Gender and Immigration on Pension Outcomes in Canada," *Canadian Public Policy* 34, no. 3 (November 2008): S59–78.

27 Béland and Myles, "Stasis Amidst Change."

PART TWO

The Economy, the Environment,
and the Federation

6 The Economy: From Innovation to Policy

MICHELLE ALEXOPOULOS AND JON COHEN

The stunning real GDP per capita increase experienced by Canadians since Confederation has enabled us to enjoy one of the highest standards of living in the world.[1] Two features of this growth are noteworthy. First, it could have turned out differently. At Confederation, Canada was economically on a par with Argentina, but the two countries took very different approaches to policy and governance. Argentina embraced protectionism and restrictive regulations, and favoured state enterprises over private ones, all of which contributed to Argentina's failure to launch. Second, while many factors have played a role in Canada's remarkable growth record, technological change stands out as critical. Innovation has enabled us to boost the quantity and the quality of capital goods and has made us much more productive at transforming inputs, such as labour and machine time, into outputs. The close of Canada's sesquicentennial presents an opportunity to pinpoint the policies that allowed us to become a technological juggernaut, to draw on them to help us fashion ones that will aid us in meeting the challenges of the future, and to insure that the gains from new innovation are widely shared by all Canadians.

Technological Change and Policy: The Views and Lessons from Past

During the second industrial revolution (approx. 1867–1918) many countries experienced waves of major technological advance, including breakthroughs in steel production, energy production, telecommunications, transportation, chemistry, and agriculture. During these years, innovations nourished one another and it became clear to scientists, inventors, and policymakers that scientific advances were the bedrock of new technologies. In Canada, this realization led to the 1916 establishment of the Canadian National Research Council, among other initiatives.

Over the next fifty years, the great innovations of the second industrial revolution came into full flower and produced one of the most technologically progressive periods ever, despite the disruptions associated with the Great Depression and the Second World War.[2] Advances in medicine transformed public health and increased life expectancy.[3] Electrification of factories reshaped the nature of work, working conditions, and wages while electrification of homes created new opportunities for the development and deployment of household appliances, new work for electricians, and new scope for housewives, now liberated from household chores, to pursue careers.[4] Automobiles allowed us to live in one place and work in another, and trucks enabled us to move goods quickly and flexibly from factories to retail outlets.

Policymakers actively facilitated these technological advances. Safety standards for household wiring were introduced by the Canadian Electrical Code, highway safety was ensured by highway traffic acts, and workplace safety standards were developed by newly created provincial Ministries of Labour. Starting in 1944, the government used research and development (R&D) tax credits to encourage innovation.[5] The National Research Council ramped up postwar funding for private sector and university research.[6] Moreover, despite various groups' opposition to the pace of innovation – disruptive technologies always create losers as well as winners[7] – politicians wisely resisted slowing the change.[8] While old jobs and whole industries were compromised by the new technologies, they also created new employment opportunities and fostered the growth of entirely new sectors. As we show using U.S. data for the 1930s, rapid technological change during the period caused substantial churning in the labour market, but did not lead to an increase in the overall level of unemployment.[9]

Innovation, of course, did not end in the 1960s. The period instead ushered in the third industrial revolution, this time associated with information and computer technologies (ICT).[10] As usual, many feared that the new innovations would eliminate jobs and, as usual, they were wrong. Some jobs did disappear and some skills were rendered obsolete, but, as in the past, these technologies also created a whole new set of employment and entrepreneurial opportunities. It is no surprise, then, to find that the unemployment rate has remained stable even as we have witnessed a jump in labour force participation. In other words, despite the usual concerns that the innovations of the ICT revolution would finally make labour redundant, they did not.

Policymakers in Canada continued to encourage innovation and helped firms and workers reap the benefits. Tri-council funding (1977–) stimulated research and innovation in universities and colleges with positive externalities for the private sector. Support for high quality public schools, affordable postsecondary education, and enlightened immigration policies contributed to the growth of a skilled workforce. Direct government R&D grants and tax incentives encouraged businesses to invest in research while reductions in trade barriers kept costs down and incentives to innovate up. It was in this environment that two homegrown technology leaders, RIM and NorTel, emerged and prospered for a time. Their fates are instructive. The technological frontier can change in an instant, which means that investment in research and development must be ongoing and the policy environment must remain friendly to innovation.[11]

Technological Change and Policy in the Present and Future

So where are we today and what can we look forward to tomorrow? Economists differ in their answers to these questions largely because, as Mark Twain pointed out, "The art of prophecy is very difficult – especially with respect to the future." Some analysts, such as Robert Gordon, believe that economically advanced economies have entered a long, dismal period of secular stagnation defined by low productivity growth and slow economic expansion. According to this view, the productivity gains of the second and third industrial revolutions have been exhausted and no comparable technological advances are likely to come along any time soon. There are others, however, who believe that when it comes to the future of technology, as Mokyr puts it, "we ain't seen nothing yet," and the period of dismal stagnation will soon be at an end.[12]

Resolution of this debate is critical for policy. If the technology pessimists are correct, then policymakers face the daunting task of trying to match the productivity gains of the past with a dwindling supply of transformative technologies. In this scenario, governments will have to increase their direct support for R&D and expand their innovation-supporting tax credits, conscious always that it will take more and more resources to achieve smaller and smaller gains. Given that Canadian productivity lags behind that of the United States, it may be possible in the short term to achieve some advances with policies that encourage foreign direct investment and facilitate additional importation of state-of-the-art technologies. But this leaves unresolved the more vex-ing problem of how Canada can maintain its prosperity as the produc-tivity gains from innovation diminish.

That's the bad news scenario. If the optimists are correct, the future looks much less gloomy – but the challenges for policymakers are no less complex. Canadians will still benefit from policies that encourage innovation at home and the adoption of state-of-the-art technologies from abroad. However, these new technologies can disrupt entire sec-tors and render obsolete a wide range of skills with serious implications for both income distribution and employment.

Exploring the Productivity Slowdown

As most economists know, productivity growth rates in many countries slowed in the early 2000s. While the data are not in dispute, the reasons for the drop are. Gordon, for example, contends that the slowdown is attributable in part to an ongoing secular decline in innovative activ-ity, halted briefly by the ICT revolution that came and went in a single decade. Others, including us, would argue that innovations come in waves of greater and lesser intensity – we've seen slowdowns before and are likely to encounter them again. As in the past, there are compel-ling signs that, once more, the wheels of innovation and productivity growth have already begun to spin.[13]

Despite Mark Twain's caution, economists and scientists are fairly good at predicting the likely path of technological change in the near future because many of tomorrow's breakthroughs are already in the blueprint or early development stages today – the subjects of confer-ences, media reports, books and articles.[14] Building on this premise, we developed in our previous work direct indicators of technological in-novation based on fluctuations in the number of new books in various fields of science and technology, showed that they tracked the commer-cialization of new technologies, and were causally linked to fluctua-tions in productivity and output. The intuition behind these measures is straightforward. Printed materials (books, pamphlets, e-books) help inform potential customers of new innovations, providing guidance for their use and maintenance so that keeping track of these materials of-fers information on the development and use of new technologies.

We draw on three sources of printed materials to examine current trends in innovation. The first is the holdings of the Library of Congress of the United States – the world's largest book depository. The second is

R.R. Bowker's books in print database that records new titles available for purchase each month from major publishers in different countries by subject and publication year. The third is Amazon's Canadian and American retail websites, which record new titles by subject. Taken together, these data confirm that the commercialization of innovations slowed in the early 2000s. But they also show a marked recovery beginning around 2010 concentrated in the areas of Artificial Intelligence (AI), robotics, web connectivity, cybersecurity, and cloud computing.

Assuming that these are the likely loci of technological change in the near future, what impact are the innovations likely to have on Canada's economy? An analysis of Canadian news articles contained in the Factiva database indicates, first, that AI and robotics are viewed as major disruptors and, second, that their impact is likely to be widespread, encompassing mining, manufacturing, financial services, wholesale and retail. With the imminent arrival of driverless cars, planes, and trucks, they will impact transportation as well. In short, it appears that the business landscape is on the verge of major change – some activities and sectors will surely disappear or be fundamentally transformed while entirely new ones, full of opportunities, will spring up.

As for jobs, a recent study by the Brookfield Institute for Innovation + Entrepreneurship suggests that 42 per cent of Canadian jobs are in jeopardy of being automated over the next 10 to 20 years, with the elderly, the young, and the less educated most impacted by the changes.[15] Lest we panic, it is important to recall that we have seen large-scale technological disruptions before, and in all cases the fear that machines were overall job destroyers turned out to be unfounded. On the other hand, complacency is also unwarranted – these disruptions both altered the kinds of skills that workers needed and reshaped the labour market as job requirements were modified to meet new work environments.

Policy Recommendations

In light of all these likely changes, what can and should policymakers do? Our first recommendation is simple – do no harm. Do not discourage competition, foreign or domestic. Do not be swayed by the vested interests of industries and workers threatened by disruption. Do not succumb to the inevitable pressures these groups will exert to restrict or otherwise hamper the importation of state-of-the-art "appropriate technology." As for grants and other forms of government support for science and technology, do not try to pick winners – let the market do that.

Always keep in mind that creative destruction is part of the growth process and must be encouraged not suppressed.[16] Our innovative potential will be fully achieved only if we allow a "thousand flowers to bloom" – the most robust will prosper.[17]

On a more constructive note, there are a number of ways that policymakers can help Canadian firms pursue cutting edge new technologies and maintain a competitive position in the global economy. Since both public and private sector R&D serve as important inputs into the creation of new ideas and technologies, continued government support for research at universities and colleges, the maintenance of R&D tax credits for firms, and the enforcement of intellectual property rights should remain priorities.[18] The expansion of grants, tax breaks, and funding for incubator and accelerator programs also makes economic sense as there is evidence that this type of assistance speeds up the conversion of good ideas into marketable technologies.[19] Cybersecurity, already important, will become more so as we transition to a digital world. At the very least, policymakers must ensure that our regulatory environment fosters secure systems. Our ability to embrace AI and the so-called "internet of things" will depend on the evolution of a congenial infrastructure and legal and regulatory framework that facilitates the fast and secure transmission of massive quantities of data.[20] This, in a sense, is just an updated version of the policies introduced a century ago to ensure the safe and rapid spread of our electricity grid and highway systems. It will also be necessary to maintain an innovation-friendly tax structure and regulatory framework to make sure that Canadian firms stay home and that firms from abroad find Canada an attractive place to invest.[21]

Disruption in labour markets will require significant attention. First, since the presence of a well-trained and skilled workforce is a magnet for high-tech investments, stepped-up investment at both the federal and provincial levels in postsecondary education and training in STEM related subjects is likely to have a substantial payoff over the medium run.[22] Similarly, as immigration can be a great source of skilled workers, and as we are likely to face skill shortages in the near future, we need to make it easy and attractive for those with the requisite training to move here.[23] To minimize the negative impact on those displaced by the new technologies, federal and provincial governments must step up investments in retraining and apprenticeship programs and enhance job search and mobility programs. For those who are unable to transition to new jobs, we, as a society, must entertain creative alternatives, including among other possibilities the introduction of basic income supplements.[24]

Less obvious but no less important, provincial governments should seriously consider redesigned curricula that introduce courses in coding and entrepreneurship at the primary and secondary school levels. Unambiguous evidence shows that honing these skills early produces large returns to both the individual and the economy.[25] In short, forward-looking policies will maximize the benefits that we as country will derive from the latest batch of transformative technologies and will, at the same time, minimize the disruptions, dislocations, and potential discontents that are likely to accompany these advances. It may not be easy to have our cake and eat it too but we need to make every effort to do so.

NOTES

1 See the "Maddison Project Database 2013" (University of Groningen), accessed April 12, 2018, https://www.rug.nl/ggdc/historicaldevelopment/maddison/releases/maddison-project-database-2013.
2 See for example Michelle Alexopoulos and Jon Cohen, "Measuring Our Ignorance, One Book at a Time: New Indicators of Technological Change, 1909–1949," *Journal of Monetary Economics* 56, no. 4 (May 1, 2009): 450–70; Michelle Alexopoulos and Jon Cohen, "The Medium Is the Measure: Technical Change and Employment, 1909–1949," *The Review of Economics and Statistics* 98, no. 4 (March 23, 2016): 792–810; Alexander J. Field, "The Most Technologically Progressive Decade of the Century," *The American Economic Review* 93, no. 4 (September 2003): 1399–413; Robert J. Gordon, *The Rise and Fall of American Growth: The U.S. Standard of Living since the Civil War*, The Princeton Economic History of the Western World (Princeton: Princeton University Press, 2016).
3 Joel Mokyr, *The Gifts of Athena: Historical Origins of the Knowledge Economy* (Princeton: Princeton University Press, 2002); Stefania Albanesi and Claudia Olivetti, "Gender Roles and Medical Progress," *Journal of Political Economy* 124, no. 3 (May 3, 2016): 650–95.
4 Jeremy Greenwood, Ananth Seshadri, and Guillaume Vandenbroucke, "The Baby Boom and Baby Bust," *American Economic Review* 95, no. 1 (March 2005): 183–207.
5 Odette Madore, "Scientific Research and Experimental Development: Tax Policy," *Current Issue Review* (Library of Parliament: Economics Division, Parliamentary Research Branch, August 31, 1998), http://publications.gc.ca/Collection-R/LoPBdP/CIR-e/899-e.pdf.

6 See National Research Council Canada, "Growing with a Nation – a Photo History of Canada's National Research Council, 1916–2016," January 21, 2016, https://www.nrc-cnrc.gc.ca/eng/about/centennial/timeline.html.

7 Gordon, *The Rise and Fall of American Growth*; Mokyr, *The Gifts of Athena*; Michelle Alexopoulos and Jon Cohen, "Volumes of Evidence: Examining Technical Change in the Last Century through a New Lens," *Canadian Journal of Economics* 44, no. 2 (May 2011): 413–50.

8 In 1984, for example, an NDP task force recommended the government cut the work week to 32 hours and grants workers decision rights regarding technological changes in the workplace that would affect their employment prospects. These recommendations were not adopted. See Robert Stephens, "Shorten Work Week, NDP Task Force Urges," *The Globe and Mail*, March 30, 1984.

9 Alexopoulos and Cohen, "The Medium Is the Measure."

10 See for example Michelle Alexopoulos, "Read All about It!! What Happens Following a Technology Shock?," *American Economic Review* 101, no. 4 (June 2011): 1144–79.

11 Indeed, some argue that poorly-planned policies which underfund private-public research and inhibit competition have contributed to Canada's more recent lacklustre productivity and innovation performance. Moreover, innovation strategies, too narrowly focused on R&D initiatives, have failed to provide substantial encouragement for the adoption of innovation-based business strategies, and the optimal redesigning of business processes, training, and marketing. See for example Andrei Sulzenko, "Canada's Innovation Conundrum: Five Years After the Jenkins Report" (Institute for Research on Public Policy, June 2016), http://irpp.org/research-studies/canadas-innovation-conundrum/; Expert Panel on Business Innovation, "Innovation and Business Strategy: Why Canada Falls Short" (Council of Canadian Academies, 2009), http://www.scienceadvice.ca/en/assessments/completed/innovation.aspx.

12 Joel Mokyr, "Is Technological Progress a Thing of the Past?," *VoxEU.Org*, September 8, 2013, https://voxeu.org/article/technological-progress-thing-past.

13 David Landes, *The Unbound Prometheus* (Cambridge, UK: Cambridge University Press, 1970); Mokyr, *The Gifts of Athena*; Michelle Alexopoulos and Jon Cohen, "Secular Stagnation, Technological Change and the Relationship with Productivity," University of Toronto Department of Economics working paper, November 2017.

14 For example, Roosevelt's 1937 committee on technological trends observed that all of the correct predictions in a 1920 issue of *Scientific American* were associated with innovations in the early stages of implementation

at the time. See "The Future as Suggested by Developments of the Past Seventy-Five Years," *The Scientific American* 123, no. 4 (October 1920): 321–5; Charles H. Townes, "Science, Technology, and Invention: Their Progress and Interactions," *Proceedings of the National Academy of Sciences* 80, no. 24 (December 1, 1983): 7679–83; "Technological Trends and National Policy Including the Social Implications of New Inventions," Report of the Subcommittee on Technology to the National Resources Committee (Washington, D.C., 1937).

15 Creig Lamb, "The Talented Mr. Robot: The Impact of Automation on Canada's Workforce" (Brookfield Institute for Innovation + Entrepreneurship, June 2016), http://brookfieldinstitute.ca/research-analysis/automation/. A 2017 report by the Department of Finance suggests a quarter of the tasks performed by Canadian workers could be displaced by automation by 2030. See Department of Finance Advisory Council on Economic Growth, "Learning Nation: Equipping Canada's Workforce with Skills for the Future" (Ottawa, December 1, 2017), https://www.budget.gc.ca/aceg-ccce/pdf/learning-nation-eng.pdf.

16 See for example Philippe Aghion, Antonin Bergeaud, Timo Boppart, Peter J. Klenow, and Huiyu Li, "Missing Growth from Creative Destruction," *Federal Reserve Bank of San Francisco Working Paper*, November 13, 2017, https://www.frbsf.org/economic-research/publications/working-papers/2017/may/; Joseph A. Schumpeter, *Capitalism, Socialism, and Democracy* (New York, London: Harper & Brothers, 1942).

17 Given that the collection, analysis, and manipulation of data are central to these new ICT technologies, policymakers (and the Canadian public) will nonetheless have to determine where to draw the line between privacy protection and economic interests.

18 For evidence of a positive relationship between R&D intensity and productivity growth, see Charles I. Jones, "Sources of U.S. Economic Growth in a World of Ideas," *American Economic Review* 92, no. 1 (March 2002): 220–39; Alexopoulos, "Read All about It!! What Happens Following a Technology Shock?" For a review of data on tax credits across countries and their impacts, see Silvia Appelt, Matej Bajgari, Chiara Criscuolo, Fernando Galindo-Rueda, "R&D Tax Incentives: Evidence on Design, Incidence and Impacts," *OECD Science, Technology and Industry Policy Papers*, no. 32 (September 10, 2016), https://www.oecd-ilibrary.org/science-and-technology/r-d-tax-incentives-evidence-on-design-incidence-and-impacts_5jlr8fldqk7j-en.

19 Similar suggestions are made in Department of Finance Advisory Council on Economic Growth, "Unlocking Innovation to Drive Scale and Growth" (Ottawa, February 6, 2017), https://www.budget.gc.ca/aceg-ccce/pdf/innovation-2-eng.pdf.

20 See Compute Canada, "Supercomputing Infrastructure: An Engine for
    Research and Innovation," *Submission to the Digital Economy Strategy
    Consultation*, June 2010, https://www.ic.gc.ca/eic/site/028.nsf/vwapj/
    Compute-Canada-Submission.pdf/$file/Compute-Canada-Submission.
    pdf; and recent advances described by the Ontario Centres of Excellence
    website, accessed April 12, 2018, http://www.oce-ontario.org/programs/
    strategic-initiatives/hpc; and Compute Canada, "Compute Canada
    Technology Briefing," November 2016, https://www.computecanada.
    ca/wp-content/uploads/2015/02/161125-Tech_Brief_PROOF_2016_
    EN_05-1.pdf.
21 For example, the regulatory environment is cited as a key reason Amazon
    chose to test Drone technology in Canada over the United States. See page
    four of Global Affairs Canada, "Invest in Canada: Canada's Robotics In-
    dustry," http://www.international.gc.ca/investors-investisseurs/assets/
    pdfs/download/Niche_Sector-Robotics.pdf.
22 See Council of Canadian Academies, "Some Assembly Required: STEM
    Skills and Canada's Economic Productivity" (Ottawa, 2015), http://public.
    eblib.com/choice/publicfullrecord.aspx?p=3432610.
23 Indeed.com found that the growth in artificial intelligence and machine
    learning job opportunities had grown by nearly 500 per cent from 2015
    to 2017, while the job seeker interest rose by only 263 per cent over the
    same period. Amira Zubairi, "Report: Canadian Job Opportunities in AI
    Have Grown by Nearly 500%," *BetaKit*, July 27, 2017, https://betakit.com/
    report-canadian-job-opportunities-in-ai-have-grown-by-nearly-500/.
24 For current research on basic income support, see the Government
    of Ontario's Basic Income pilot website: "Ontario Basic Income Pi-
    lot," Ontario.ca, accessed July 6, 2018, https://www.ontario.ca/page/
    ontario-basic-income-pilot.
25 See Council of Canadian Academies, "Some Assembly Required."

7 Natural Resources, Federalism, and the Canadian Economy

KATHRYN HARRISON

The export of natural resources has been central to Canada's economy since European contact, from codfish and beaver pelts pre-Confederation, to forest products and wheat in Canada's first century, to fossil fuels in recent decades. Natural resources have held a place of prominence not only in the economy, but also in the federation as federal and provincial governments alike have relied heavily on resources as a source of both government revenues and job creation. While that has given rise to occasional tensions, intergovernmental conflicts have been a minor inconvenience of prosperity.

The vision for Canada's economy and federation for the next fifty years is considerably less promising. Canada has come to rely increasingly on oil and gas exports even as the international community has agreed that climate change requires urgent reduction in fossil fuel consumption. Action to mitigate climate change represents an existential threat to an economy heavily dependent on fossil fuels. Looking ahead, federal and provincial governments can be expected to clash over the pace of transition away from fossil fuels and over distribution of associated costs, potentially within the context of a shrinking economy.

History of Natural Resource Exports

Harold Innis documented the many ways export of raw "staples" from the Canadian colonies to the European metropolis influenced economic and political development of our settler society.[1] The popularity of beaver fur hats among wealthy Europeans prompted French and English fur traders to move ever further north and west along a system of interconnected rivers and lakes. Associated trade with Indigenous peoples brought disruptive technologies and devastating diseases to traditional communities. As European fashion moved on from beaver fur, the colonial project of resource exploitation also moved on. Demand for timber prompted further geographic expansion. Following Confederation, the Dominion Lands Act took advantage of lands gained (through questionable treaties) from First Nations to promote European immigration via homesteading. In turn, Western settlement gave rise to exports of wheat and other agricultural commodities.

Canada's natural resource exports have evolved over time, from codfish and beaver pelts in the early days of European settlement to lumber, pulp, potash, and agricultural products in Canada's first century, and more recently to oil and gas. However, one pattern has remained constant: resources have been exported in raw or minimally processed form from the Canadian "hinterland" to a more populous "heartland," originally Europe but later the United States.

Canadian oil was first discovered in Ontario in 1857, and natural gas in New Brunswick two years later. However, oil and gas did not become significant exports until after the Second World War. As North Americans' demand for oil grew, fortuitously so did Canada's reserves. With the discovery of oil at Leduc, Alberta, in 1947, the Canadian oil industry moved west.[2] Conventional oil production steadily increased, hitting one million barrels per day about the time of Canada's centennial. It has fluctuated between 1.0 and 1.5 million barrels/day since then. As both oil and gas increased in value, they surpassed forest products as Canada's leading resource export by the mid-1980s.

In 1967, economically-viable extraction of oil from the tar sands of Northern Alberta was still largely a dream of industry executives and provincial politicians. Great Canadian Oil Sands' first upgrader was under construction, offering the promise of 45,000 barrels per day.[3] Tar sands production increased from the 1970s onward, but it was not until the 2000s that a combination of technological innovation, favourable government policies, and rising oil prices yielded a dramatic increase in production.[4] Production of unconventional oil overtook conventional in 2009. As conventional reserves decline, the tar sands are expected to provide virtually all future growth in Canadian production.

Increasing oil production has largely been in the service of exports, virtually all heading to the United States. From 1990 to 2015, production increased by a factor of 2.3, but exports increased by double that. The fraction of Canadian oil production that is exported increased from 39 per cent to 78 per cent.[5] Fossil fuels surpassed motor vehicles as

Canada's leading export in 2007 and maintained that lead until 2016, when the decline in global oil prices reduced the value of Canada's oil exports despite growing volumes.[6]

Over time it has become increasingly energy-intensive to produce Canada's oil. In the earliest days, production was free-flowing. As reservoir pressure declined, pumping required modest energy input. However, the shift to tar sands and *in situ* heavy oil production presents much greater challenges. Bitumen must be extracted from tar sands with steam and chemicals, and the resulting tarry product requires further upgrading to produce a "synthetic crude" suitable for processing in a conventional refinery. *In situ* production similarly requires heat and solvents to extract heavy oil from deeper deposits via horizontally drilled wells. Energy requirements for extraction and upgrading typically are met by burning natural gas, which has significantly increased greenhouse gas emissions per barrel of oil produced.

Federalism and Natural Resources

At Confederation, provincial governments were granted ownership of "Crown lands" within their borders. The resources thereon were seen as an important source of revenues for provincial governments, in compensation for more limited taxation powers relative to the federal government. As owners of Crown lands, provincial governments have authority to either conserve or develop natural resources on their lands, including forests, wildlife, minerals, and hydro-electric resources. Moreover, even as Crown lands have been ceded to private owners, provincial governments typically have retained ownership of subsurface minerals, thus ensuring that oil and gas reserves also belong to the provinces. Provincial governments historically have been jealous of their jurisdiction over natural resources for two reasons. Resource royalties are an important source of provincial revenues. Perhaps even more importantly, exploitation of natural resources is a valuable source of economic development, job creation, and thus electoral support.

The Canadian constitution grants the federal government various sources of overlapping authority concerning natural resources, including taxation, international trade, fisheries, navigation, and "interprovincial works and undertakings" such as pipelines. It is thus standard for any resource development to be governed by both provincial and federal laws. Not surprisingly, overlap has generated occasional intergovernmental conflict. Federal-provincial conflict was particularly heated during the energy crises of the 1970s and early 1980s.[7] As the OPEC embargo increased the price of oil imports on which Eastern Canadian consumers relied, the federal government responded by capping the price of oil. Albertans were outraged by a federal policy that effectively required that they cross-subsidize Eastern Canadian consumers, despite the fact that since 1961 consumers west of the Ottawa River had cross-subsidized Alberta oil producers because the National Oil Policy created a protected market for Alberta's oil. Tensions between Alberta and the federal government were exacerbated by the introduction of the National Energy Program in 1980. These disputes were largely resolved by the mid-1980s through a gradual deregulation of domestic oil prices and adoption of a constitutional amendment (Section 92A) that reaffirmed provincial authority with respect to Crown resources, including oil and gas.

Tensions flared again over renewed federal environmental assertiveness in the late 1980s, which raised the prospect of federal intervention in provincial resource developments. Of particular note were conflicts between the federal government and the provinces of Saskatchewan and Alberta concerning federal environmental impact assessments of provincial dams. By the early 1990s, the federal and provincial governments resolved their differences through joint environmental assessments and, more generally, a return to federal deference to the provinces.[8]

Alberta's growing oil-driven wealth has also presented challenges in a federation committed to equalization of provincial governments' ability to deliver services to their citizens. Although equalization payments are often mischaracterized as a transfer of wealth from Alberta to other provinces, in fact equalization is financed by the federal government with national tax revenues. When Alberta's greater wealth created a tax and spending burden for the federal government, the issue was resolved by adjusting the equalization formula to exclude resource royalties, with the implication of greater inequality among provinces.

It warrants emphasis that each of these intergovernmental conflicts was a function of abundance. As Crown lands yielded valuable resources, federal and provincial governments competed to collect and/ or distribute the spoils.

Prospects for the Canadian Economy in a Carbon-Constrained World

Climate change presents challenges to Canada as a result of rising seas, melting permafrost, and extreme storms. However, the international community's commitment to limit climate change to 2°C also presents a fundamental challenge for Canada's economy. Canadian politicians' and industry leaders' rebranding of oil and gas as the "energy industry" may succeed in redirecting attention away from climate change, but it cannot change the fact that fossil fuels release energy *by* producing carbon dioxide. Used as intended, fossil fuels cause climate change.

As one of the countries with the highest carbon emissions per capita in the world, and with emissions still increasing, Canadians face a particularly acute challenge in reducing our own emissions. Canadian households and business alike are accustomed to inexpensive fossil fuel-derived energy. A more immediate challenge is presented by our export-oriented fossil fuel industry, however. By international agreement, emissions from the combustion of exported oil and gas are the responsibility of destination countries in which they are burned. However, emissions associated with extraction and upgrading prior to export are Canada's responsibility. These emissions within Canada's borders have increased dramatically in response to both the growing scale of production and the shift to unconventional oil, which requires more energy and thus greater emissions to produce. Oil production alone accounted for three-quarters of the growth in Canada's carbon emissions from 1990 to 2014.[9] Moreover, as illustrated by Figure 7.1, oil and gas production is the one sector from which emissions are projected to continue growing.

In 2016, the federal government reached an agreement with the provinces (except Saskatchewan and Manitoba) called the Pan-Canadian

Figure 7.1. Trends in Canadian Greenhouse Gas Emissions, by Sector (MT CO_2eq/yr)[10]

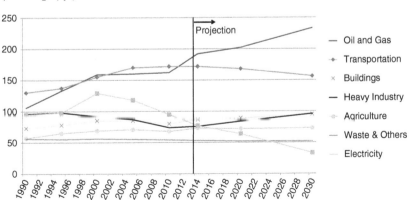

Framework on Clean Growth and Climate Change. The framework commits Canada to many laudable measures, including an accelerated phase-out of coal-fired power and a national carbon price. However, the plan is projected to fall short of meeting Canada's 2030 target under the international Paris Agreement by an amount roughly equivalent to projected growth from the tar sands. The challenge to domestic emissions reductions presented by the oil and gas industry will only grow as Canada's targets become more demanding over time.

Thus far, I have focused my discussion on Canada's emissions. However, as other countries seek to meet their emissions targets, global fossil fuel consumption will decline. When that occurs, there are two reasons to anticipate that demand for Canada's oil will be among the first to go. First, as international demand declines so too will the price of oil, thus crowding our relatively expensive oil out of the market. Canadians, and especially Albertans, have already experienced the impact of declining oil prices on the competitiveness of Canada's unconventional oil. Although the drop in global oil prices in 2014 reflected growing supply rather than declining demand, the effect of international climate change mitigation will be much the same for Canadian producers. Second, as Canada's own extraction emissions are curtailed or taxed, the associated costs will cause the price of Canada's oil to increase, further hindering global competitiveness.

Modelling global oil demand according to different scenarios suggests that the impacts on the Canadian economy could be dramatic indeed. The International Energy Agency (IEA) anticipates that if the international community actually met its goal to limit climate change to 2°C, global oil demand must peak by 2020. McGlade and Ekins project that in the 2°C scenario, demand for Canada's bitumen would disappear entirely by 2020.[11] In reality, international commitments made thus far under the Paris Agreement fall well short of what is needed to achieve the 2°C target. However, even under the existing Paris scenario, the IEA anticipates that global demand for heavy oil and bitumen will grow just under one million barrels per day by 2030, less than half of what was expected pre-Paris.

Neither scenario is favourable for Canada. Adherence to the Paris target of 2°C would decimate Canada's oil industry almost immediately. And even the first steps locked into the Paris Agreement suggest much lower growth in demand for unconventional fuels than Canada has been counting on. The latter scenario will also entail significantly greater climate change, with resulting costs to the Canadian landscape and economy.

Implications for the Canadian Federation

The combined challenge of domestic emissions reductions and declining global demand for Canada's fossil fuel exports suggests that federal-provincial dynamics in the next fifty years will be very different from past struggles over the wealth derived from natural resources. Figure 7.2 illustrates the disparity in per-capita emissions in different provinces, which underscores the potential for emissions reductions to have disparate costs across Canada.

The first and most obvious implication for federal-provincial relations is disagreement over the appropriate level of ambition for Canadian climate action. Such disagreement is hardly new. A long-standing norm of federal-provincial consensus in Canadian environmental policy has allowed Alberta to wield an effective veto over national climate policy for more than two decades. However, if the federal government and less emissions-intensive provinces are now serious about climate action, that level of conflict can be expected to grow over time. It is no accident that Saskatchewan, which has the highest per-capita emissions among Canadian provinces, is leading the charge against the Pan-Canadian climate plan and federal carbon tax. They have been joined by the newly elected Conservative government in Ontario, and to a

Figure 7.2. Canadian Per Capita Emissions (2014) by Province/Territory

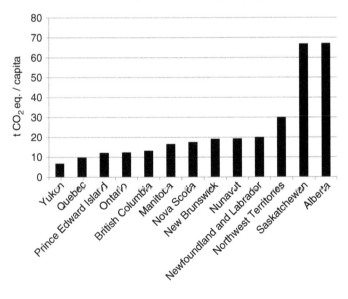

lesser degree the NDP government in Alberta, though stronger opposition to a national carbon price can be expected should the next provincial election yield a change in government in that province as well.

Second, as provincial governments led by Quebec and British Columbia move forward with carbon pricing, interprovincial conflict is likely to increase as hard-won emissions reductions in those provinces are undone by emissions growth in Alberta and Saskatchewan. The provinces are already at war over pipeline infrastructure. Quebecers adamantly opposed the now-defunct Energy East proposal, while the Green Party-backed NDP government in British Columbia has vowed to use all constitutional tools at its disposal to oppose the Kinder Morgan pipeline expansion.

Last, one can only begin to imagine the federal-provincial conflicts that will emerge should Canada fail to transition its economy away from reliance on fossil fuels in time. Conflicts over oil revenues will pale in comparison to those associated with a shrinking economy as markets for Canada's oil disappear.

Conclusion

Canada's centennial was a time of great optimism with a prevailing message that the next century would be Canada's to embrace. Despite the celebratory tone of Canada 150 events, Canada's economic future is shrouded in uncertainty amid growing climate change. Fifty years on, we can ill-afford complacency. Yet the government of Canada is doubling down on the expansion of oil exports, even as it dons the moral mantle of climate leadership on the world stage. Canada is locking in a deep economic dependence on oil, even as its economy becomes more vulnerable to a much-needed decline in international demand.

A critical but seldom-acknowledged question is what will replace oil as Canada's leading export. In the past, Canada has moved with relative ease from one resource to the next: wheat and forest products replaced trade in furs and cod, and these were later supplanted by oil. There is no next natural resource on the horizon. Canada's landmass may be conducive to wind and solar farms, but solar power can't be loaded for export on a ship to Asia. With the exception of modest untapped reserves of hydro-power, Canada does not have a comparative advantage in *clean* energy.

The time has come for Canada to move from reliance on exports of raw material to the innovation of its highly-educated citizens. There is little time to spare if we hope to ensure both a habitable planet and domestic prosperity for Canada's bicentennial.

NOTES

1 Harold A. Innis, *The Fur Trade in Canada: An Introduction to Canadian Economic History* (New Haven, CT: Yale University Press, 1930); Harold A. Innis, *The Cod Fisheries: The History of an International Economy* (New Haven, CT: Yale University Press, 1940).

2 Statistics Canada, "Oil and Gas Extraction, 2016," October 6, 2017, http://www.statcan.gc.ca/daily-quotidien/171006/dq171006b-eng.htm.

3 David S. Boyer, "Canadian North – Emerging Giant," *National Geographic* 134, no. 1 (1968): 1–43.

4 Ian Urquhart, *Costly Fix: Power, Politics, and Nature in the Tar Sands* (Toronto: University of Toronto Press, 2018).

5 Calculations based on Statistics Canada, "CANSIM 126-0001: Crude Oil and Equivalent, Monthly Supply and Disposition," February 12, 2018, https://www150.statcan.gc.ca/t1/tbl1/en/tv.action?pid=2510001401.

6 Calculations based on Statistics Canada, "CANSIM 228-0059: International Merchandise Trade by Commodity," April 23, 2018, https://www150.statcan.gc.ca/t1/tbl1/en/tv.action?pid=1210000101. Fossil fuel exports includes crude oil and bitumen, natural gas, and refined petroleum products.

7 John Richards and Larry Pratt, *Prairie Capitalism: Power and Influence in the New West* (Toronto: McClelland and Stewart, 1979).

8 Kathryn Harrison, *Passing the Buck: Federalism and Canadian Environmental Policy* (Vancouver, BC: UBC Press, 1996).

9 Environment and Climate Change Canada, "National Inventory Report 1990–2016: Greenhouse Gas Sources and Sinks in Canada," Canada's Submission to the United Nations Framework Convention on Climate Change, accessed July 15, 2018, https://www.canada.ca/en/environment-climate-change/services/climate-change/greenhouse-gas-emissions/inventory.html.

10 Environment and Climate Change Canada, "Canada's 2016 Greenhouse Gas Emissions Reference Case," December 9, 2016, https://www.canada.ca/en/environment-climate-change/services/climate-change/publications/2016-greenhouse-gas-emissions-case.html.

11 Christophe McGlade and Paul Ekins, "The Geographical Distribution of Fossil Fuels Unused When Limiting Global Warming to 2°C," *Nature* 517, no. 7533 (January 2015): 187–90.

8 Environmental Policy Transformations and Canada at 150

JENNIFER WINTER

Like all policy areas, environmental, energy, and natural resources policies have transformed significantly during Canada's history. These policy evolutions are a result of changing values and knowledge. In addition, four underlying features of Canadian policy (federal, provincial and territorial) have strongly influenced energy and environmental policy, and to a lesser extent, natural resources policy. These features are the division of powers between the federal and provincial governments over natural resources; the regional nature of natural resource endowments; the United States' prominence as a trading partner; and the fact that the Constitution is silent on the environment.[1]

The division of powers means that provinces have control over their natural resources, while the federal government regulates trade and offshore development.[2] This overlapping jurisdiction has historically led to inter-jurisdictional and interregional tension. The regional nature of natural resource endowments – and in particular energy endowments – has led to significant policy divergence between federal or provincial policies, and between policy actions of individual provinces. At times, federal policy has benefited one region at the expense of another. The regional endowments have also significantly affected economic development, which in turn influences policy direction. The United States' dominance among Canada's trading partners has resulted in considerable policy cooperation between the two nations. However, this strong economic relationship means there are many instances where Canada is reluctant to engage in policy action without the cooperation of the United States. Finally, the Constitution's silence on the environment means the environment is another area of shared jurisdiction among Canadian governments, with the associated tensions that entails.[3] All these combined mean energy and environmental policy and politics in Canada have been, and continue to be, controversial.[4]

More recently, Canadian energy and environmental policy has become inextricably intertwined. Central themes of modern policy discussion and development include protecting the environment, debate about whether Canada's continued use and production of fossil fuels is sustainable, and using energy policy to achieve environmental goals. With this in mind, the rest of this chapter will explore the issue of climate policy as Canada's pre-eminent environmental policy challenge, which is likely to define energy and environmental policy for the foreseeable future.

Current and Future Policy Challenges

In terms of environmental policy, first and foremost in the minds of many Canadians is the challenge of climate change and the appropriate response to climate change at the national and subnational levels. Climate policies vary by jurisdiction: in addition to the national emissions reduction target, the majority of provinces and territories have their own targets, with varying stringency. The federal backstop carbon price notwithstanding, each province and territory also has its own approach to achieving its emissions targets. The approaches differ in pace, stringency, amount of overall policy action, and the level of political will. For example, while Alberta introduced a broad-based carbon tax in 2017, Albertans are concerned about the costs of the tax (and other policies) on emissions-intensive and trade-exposed sectors of the economy, and the associated leakage of economic activity and greenhouse gas emissions to other jurisdictions. This prompted a second policy, the Carbon Competitiveness Incentive (introduced at the end of 2017), which gives firms defined as emissions-intensive and trade-exposed emissions credits based on facility production and a product- or facility-specific emissions benchmark.[5]

The environmental economics literature offers some insight into the political and policy challenges facing Canadian governments in their response to climate change.[6] Broadly speaking, there are three types of environmental problems (in economics parlance, market failures) that justify government intervention: externalities, which are direct, unintentional, and uncompensated consequences imposed on others that are external to the decision process of the actor; public goods, which are goods shared by all and owned by no one; and the tragedy of the commons, which describes individually rational actions that result in a socially undesirable outcome.[7] The issue of climate change and the anthropogenic emissions that contribute to climate change can be expressed as all or any of these three classic environmental problems. For externalities, production processes (and human activity more generally) create emissions as a by-product, with negative consequences locally and globally. For public goods, the environment (clean atmosphere, biodiversity, etc.) itself can be considered a public good; social benefits are greater than individual private benefits, leading to under-provision of environmental quality[8] and free-riding. And for the tragedy of the commons, each country benefits from reducing greenhouse gas emissions and reducing the concentration of greenhouse gasses (GHGs) in the atmosphere, thereby reducing the probability of dangerous climate change. However, because each country's efforts to reduce emissions benefit the rest of the world and is costly to itself, governments have strong incentives to free-ride on the efforts of others.

Differences between private and social benefits, or private and social costs, give rise to these market failures and create scope for government intervention. Again, the environmental literature gives insight into the appropriate (market-based) government action to correct each environmental problem.[9] In the case of positive or negative externalities, getting prices right through taxes or subsidies means that actors imposing consequences on others will internalize the cost (benefit) of those consequences and achieve the socially optimal outcome. In the case of environmental quality as a public good, the incentive to free ride means there is effectively no market demand curve for pollution control. The role of government policy is to fill in this missing demand curve, via requiring a fixed quantity of pollution control or setting a fixed price on pollution. Finally, for the tragedy of the commons, the role for government is to assign property rights over the "commons." In the case of the environment, government can, for example, allocate the right to pollute through emissions permits. However, it is important to note that both the undersupply of public goods and the tragedy of the commons are collective action problems: a group as a whole is better off if all contribute to the common good, but each individual (person or state) has an incentive to freeride. This emphasizes the political difficulty of implementing policy changes to address the challenge of climate change, especially in inter-jurisdictional or multinational discussions.

Until recently, a fundamental question in Canada was whether concrete action should be taken at all.[10] This was in recognition of the fact that Canada was and is a marginal contributor to global greenhouse gas emissions, contributing only 1.9 per cent of global emissions in 2005 and 1.6 per cent in 2013.[11] A second consideration is that recent research suggests some countries – particularly wealthy ones – will benefit from some amount of global warming via increased economic productivity; Canada is one of these.[12] That is not to say that climate change will not be costly to Canada; the National Roundtable on the Environment and the Economy estimated that the economic costs of climate change in Canada (in 2006 dollars) would be CDN $5 billion annually in 2020, increasing to between $21 and $43 billion per year in 2050.[13] A third consideration is the costs Canada will impose on itself to meet its 2030 target of 523 million tonnes of CO_2-equivalent (CO_2e) emissions, or 30 per cent below 2005 emissions, and subsequent targets. Reducing emissions, whether by pricing, regulation, or other policy mechanisms, is costly. Based on Canada's 2015 emissions intensity of 0.35 million tonnes CO_2e per billion dollars of GDP, meeting Canada's 2030 target without reducing the emissions intensity of output would require shrinking the Canadian economy by 28 per cent. This is an unreasonable scenario, but it underscores the challenge Canada faces in balancing emissions reductions and maintaining economic growth and prosperity. The required emissions-intensity change to meet the target, with a 1.7 per cent economic growth rate, is from 0.35 to 0.19 million tonnes CO_2e per billion dollars of GDP.

A fourth consideration is the distribution of burden across provinces and territories. As Figure 8.1 shows, there are substantial differences in emissions – both gross and per capita – across provinces and territories. Higher-emission jurisdictions will necessarily bear a higher burden of emissions reductions, even in the presence of neutral policy which treats all sources of emissions the same. This will have corresponding impacts on economic activity, with consequences for the distribution of burden. Policy design has an important role to play to minimize these costs, particularly when considering the role of revenue raised through climate policies.[14]

A fifth policy issue is competitiveness and carbon leakage. Implementing carbon pricing or emissions reduction regulations will expose portions of the Canadian economy to higher costs not faced by competitors, making Canadian firms less competitive globally. As a result, economic activity could decrease or relocate to international jurisdictions, imposing economic costs on Canada and potentially increasing overall global emissions, depending on the environmental regulations in place in other jurisdictions which absorb the economic activity. The emissions intensity and trade exposure[15] of industries is a primary determinant of potential competitiveness impacts from climate policy.[16] In the absence of similar policy action from other jurisdictions, stringent climate

Figure 8.1. Total and Per Capita Emissions, by Province and Territory, 2015[17]

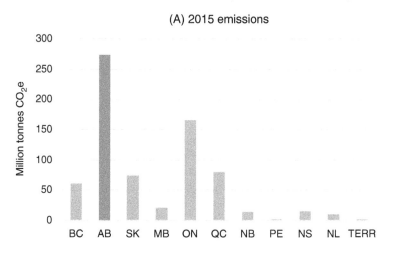

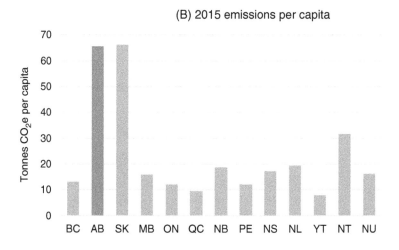

policies in Canada will have high costs and little benefit. The major impacts can be mitigated by output-based pricing schemes such as the one implemented in Alberta in late 2017 or the scheme included in the federal backstop. A related concern is that emissions-intensive and trade-exposed sectors are concentrated in Alberta, Saskatchewan, and to a lesser extent, Manitoba. This exacerbates the issue of burden-sharing and overall impact on specific provincial economies.

The issues described above underscore the collective action problem the globe faces; this collective action problem is replicated and exacerbated in subnational jurisdictions like provinces, where the benefits of action are even more diffuse. The combination of Canada's limited ability to affect global emissions and the minimal actions taken by other countries means the choice to engage in policies to reduce emissions is primarily a moral one. That said, it behooves Canadians to ensure their governments enact the most cost-effective policy solutions to this challenge, in order to meet environmental policy objectives with the least cost to the Canadian economy.

More recently, the policy debate has turned to how much action Canada should take, and the stringency of the resultant policies, given what other countries are doing (or not). The considerations driving these policy choices are the same as those enumerated above for whether to even act. In 2009, the National Roundtable on the Environment and the Economy estimated that in order to meet Canada's 2020 and 2050 targets (20 per cent and 65 per cent below 2006 levels, respectively), the national carbon price would need to be CDN $50 per tonne of CO_2e in 2015, rising to $100 in 2020, and $200 after 2025.[18] More recent modelling suggests the price needs to start at $30 per tonne, increasing to $200 by 2030, and ultimately to $300 to meet the 2050 target.[19] A 2016 study indicates a nation-wide carbon tax of $30 per tonne in 2016, rising to $110 in 2030, will leave Canada 50 to 80 million tonnes short of its 2030 target.[20] Current carbon pricing, shown in Figure 8.2, is below this threshold, though in line with estimates of the social cost of carbon by 2022. The social cost of carbon is a dollar measure of the incremental damages per tonne of increased emissions globally (or, correspondingly, the incremental benefit per tonne of decreased emissions). Of note is that in 2016, Environment and Climate Change Canada estimated the social cost of carbon to be CDN $55 per tonne (2012 dollars) in 2030 and $75 in 2050 (2012 dollars), both below the price required to meet Canada's targets.[21] This demonstrates the clear policy gap between goals and actions, which will need to be addressed either through increasing carbon prices to meet the 2020 and 2030 targets, introducing additional (and likely more costly) complementary policies,[22] purchasing international offsets, a combination of all three options, or giving up on emissions reduction targets as a policy goal. Current modelling by Environment and Climate Change Canada suggests that the Pan Canadian Framework – which includes the carbon tax and regulatory changes – will result in emissions of 567 million tonnes of CO_2e in 2030; the additional 44-million-tonne reduction to meet the target will come from other policy actions.[23]

Conclusions

Canada is taking increasingly stringent actions in its efforts to reduce emissions and prevent climate change. With few exceptions, market-based policies such as carbon taxes or cap-and-trade systems are the best way to approach this problem. And while there is a role for additional complementary policies, not all policies are created equal; we must guard ourselves against the temptation to enact policies that are politically popular (or at least politically more popular) but more

Figure 8.2. Current (circa 2019) Canadian Carbon Pricing Policies [24, 25]

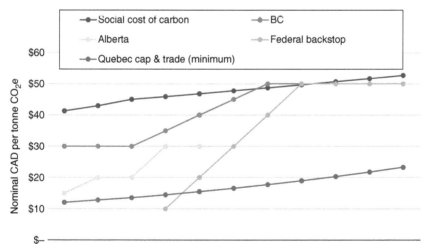

costly and less transparent. This is particularly important when thinking about election cycles and the political acceptability of climate policy such as carbon taxes. At the end of the day, Canadians should focus on the environmental problems we are trying to solve, and design policy instruments that address each problem individually.

NOTES

1 Jennifer Winter, "Making Energy Policy: The Canadian Experience," in *Meeting the Paris Mandate: A Cross-National Comparison of Energy Policy-Making*, ed. Patrice Geoffron, Lorna A. Greening, and Raphael Heffron (Springer-Verlag, forthcoming).

2 Water is an area of shared federal-provincial jurisdiction; see Government of Canada, "Water Governance and Legislation: Shared Responsibility," accessed July 16, 2018, https://www.canada.ca/en/environment-climate-change/services/water-overview/governance-legislation/shared-responsibility.html.

3 The fact the environment is not included in the Constitution also means that any federal or provincial environmental actions must fit within the defined constitutional limits, or limits determined through the courts. This is why Saskatchewan's constitutional challenge of the federal backstop is unlikely to be successful; see Nathalie Chalifour and Stewart Elgie, "Brad Wall's Carbon-Pricing Fight Is Constitutional Hot Air," *The Globe and Mail*, June 14, 2017, https://www.theglobeandmail.com/opinion/brad-walls-carbon-pricing-fight-is-constitutional-hot-air/article35297947/. This is also an interesting example of a province using opposition to a federal policy action to expand its jurisdiction.

4 See G. Bruce Doern and Monica Gattinger, *Power Switch: Energy Regulatory Governance in the Twenty-First Century* (Toronto: University of Toronto Press, 2003).

5 For an overview of the principles behind these output based subsidies, see Sarah Dobson, G. Kent Fellows, Trevor Tombe, and Jennifer Winter, "The Ground Rules for Effective OBAs: Principles for Addressing Carbon-Pricing Competitiveness Concerns through the Use of Output-Based Allocations," *The School of Public Policy Publications* 10, no. 17 (2017): 1–25. For specific details on the system itself, see Government of Alberta, "Carbon Competitiveness Incentive Regulation," accessed May 10, 2018, https://www.alberta.ca/carbon-competitiveness-incentive-regulation.aspx.

6 See Nathaniel O. Keohane and Sheila M. Olmstead, *Markets and the Environment*, 2nd ed. (Washington, D.C.: Island Press, 2016).
7 The tragedy of the commons concept was introduced by William Forster Lloyd in 1833 and made mainstream by Garett Hardin, "The Tragedy of the Commons," *Science* 162, no. 3859 (December 1968): 1243–8.
8 The quality of the environment can be thought of as a good like any other. Alternatively, the environment can be thought of as a good, while the quality of the environment is a valued characteristic that can be under-provided (quality is lower than desired).
9 While market-based policies are not always appropriate, in the vast majority of circumstances they will be the lowest cost and most effective policy instruments. For more detail, see Keohane and Olmstead, *Markets and the Environment*, chapters 8 and 9.
10 It is important to note that despite perception that the Harper government took little or no action on the environmental file, there was policy change through regulation. These regulatory changes, however, did little to lower emissions and were insufficient to meet Canada's emission reduction targets.
11 See Environment and Climate Change Canada, "Global Greenhouse Gas Emissions," Canadian Environmental Sustainability Indicators, March 16, 2012, https://www.canada.ca/en/environment-climate-change/services/environmental-indicators/global-greenhouse-gas-emissions.html.
12 See Marshall Burke, Solomon M. Hsiang, and Edward Miguel, "Global Non-Linear Effect of Temperature on Economic Production," *Nature* 527, no. 7577 (November 2015): 235–9.
13 See National Round Table on the Environment and the Economy (Canada), "Paying the Price: The Economic Impacts of Climate Change for Canada," Climate Prosperity (Ottawa, 2011), http://nrt-trn.ca/climate/climate-prosperity/the-economic-impacts-of-climate-change-for-canada/paying-the-price.
14 For more on this, see Canada's Ecofiscal Commission, "Choose Wisely: Options and Trade-Offs in Recycling Carbon Pricing Revenues," April 2016, https://ecofiscal.ca/reports/choose-wisely-options-trade-offs-recycling-carbon-pricing-revenues/; Dale Beugin, Richard Lipsey, Christopher Ragan, France St-Hilaire, and Vincent Thivierge, "Provincial Carbon Pricing and Household Fairness" (Canada's Ecofiscal Commission, April 2016), https://ecofiscal.ca/reports/provincial-carbon-pricing-household-fairness/; and Sarah Dobson and G. Kent Fellows, "Big and Little Feet: A Comparison of Provincial Level Consumption- and

Production-Based Emissions Footprints," *The School of Public Policy Publications* 10, no. 23 (September 2017): 1–43.

15 Trade exposure typically refers to how much firms trade with other jurisdictions, as trade limits their ability to pass increased costs along to customers.

16 For more detail, see Dobson et al., "The Ground Rules for Effective OBAs"; Beugin et al., "Provincial Carbon Pricing and Household Fairness"; Dave Sawyer and Seton Stiebert, "Output-Based Pricing: Theory and Practice in the Canadian Context" (Canada's Ecofiscal Commission and EnviroEconomics, December 2017), https://ecofiscal.ca/reports/output-based-pricing-theory-practice-canadian-context/.

17 Environment and Climate Change Canada, *National Inventory Report 1990–2016: Greenhouse Gas Sources and Sinks in Canada* (Ottawa: 2018), https://www.canada.ca/en/environment-climate-change/services/climate-change/greenhouse-gas-emissions/inventory.html; Statistics Canada, "CANSIM: 051-0001 - Estimates of Population, by Age Group and Sex for July 1, Canada, Provinces and Territories," October 31, 2017, http://www5.statcan.gc.ca/cansim/a26?lang=eng&id=510001.

18 See National Round Table on the Environment and the Economy, "Achieving 2050: A Carbon Pricing Policy for Canada" (Ottawa, 2009), http://nrt-trn.ca/wp-content/uploads/2011/08/carbon-pricing-advisory-note-eng.pdf.

19 See Mark Jaccard, Mikela Hein, and Tiffany Vass, "Is Win-Win Possible? Can Canada's Government Achieve Its Paris Commitment ... and Get Re-Elected?" (Simon Fraser University, September 20, 2016), http://rem-main.rem.sfu.ca/papers/jaccard/Jaccard-Hein-Vass%20CdnClimatePol%20EMRG-REM-SFU%20Sep%2020%202016.pdf.

20 See Chris Bataille and Dave Sawyer, "Canadian Carbon Pricing Pathways: The Economic and Emission Outcomes of Leading Policies" (Deep Decarbonization Pathways Canada and Canadians for Clean Prosperity, September 2016), https://drive.google.com/file/d/0B9FT5KrVwYmwY3A2RlpaTDM0N2M/view.

21 Environment and Climate Change Canada's estimates of the social cost of carbon are global, rather than the cost of Canada of marginal emissions. See Environment and Climate Change Canada, "Technical Update to Environment Canada's Social Cost of Carbon Estimates," March 2016, http://ec.gc.ca/cc/default.asp?lang=En&n=BE705779-1.

22 For more detail on the role of complementary policies, see Canada's Ecofiscal Commission, "Supporting Carbon Pricing: How to Identify Policies That Genuinely Complement an Economy-Wide Carbon Price,"

    June 2017, https://ecofiscal.ca/reports/supporting-carbon-pricing-complementary-policies/.

23 See Environment and Climate Change Canada, "National Inventory Report 1990–2016: Greenhouse Gas Sources and Sinks in Canada," Canada's Submission to the United Nations Framework Convention on Climate Change, accessed July 15, 2018, https://www.canada.ca/en/environment-climate-change/services/climate-change/greenhouse-gas-emissions/inventory.html.

24 Inflation of 2 per cent assumed for the cap and trade minimum and social cost of carbon.

25 Ontario implemented its cap and trade system in January 2017, linked with Quebec later that year, and cancelled it in July 2018.

9 The Environment as an Urban Policy Issue in Canada

MATTI SIEMIATYCKI

For the first time in human history, over half of the world's population lives in cities. Despite its geographic size and global reputation for pristine natural environments, Canada is an especially urban nation. Upwards of 80 per cent of Canadians live in cities, with more than one-third residing in just three urban agglomerations – Toronto, Montreal, and Vancouver.

Canada is a country that has steadily urbanized since confederation, a time when over four out of every five Canadians lived in rural areas. Urbanization took off after the Second World War and largely stabilized by the 1970s.[1] Canada's centennial thus took place in a human geographic landscape that was in the midst of a dramatic transformation. The rapidity of that transformation outpaced the policy and fiscal capacity to respond, and we are living with that legacy at the sesquicentennial.

It is important that Canadians consider the complex relationship between cities and the natural environment. Cities are critical engines of economic growth, production, innovation, culture, and prosperity. Yet the activities that take place in cities and make them vibrant and prosperous – such as hypermobility, density, and commercial and industrial activity – are energy-intensive and in many cases highly polluting. According to UN Habitat, nearly 80 per cent of all energy resources globally are consumed in cities, while cities generate over 60 per cent of the carbon dioxide emissions that contribute to climate change.[2] Through the daily activities of individual residents and industrial processing, cities also consume large amounts of water and produce large amounts of solid waste.

Localized air, water, waste, and soil pollution emitted in cities causes significant health hazards and premature death, with great disparities between wealthy and poor citizens. And the onset of climate change is costing cities, with more urban areas regularly experiencing major floods, wildfires, and, especially in Canada's north, structural instability caused by thawing permafrost.

Given their intensity of resource usage and susceptibility to environmental degradation, cities are critical sites for environmental sustainability and can illuminate the challenges and opportunities of achieving it. This chapter identifies the urban conditions that contribute to intensive resource consumption and pollution, and examines how policy and market interventions can play a role in improving the sustainability of cities.

Understanding the Sustainability of Cities

According to a landmark study by Chris Kennedy and his colleagues, the sustainability of cities "depends to a large extent on how they obtain, share, and manage their energy and material resources."[3] The environmental sustainability of cities is deeply connected with their spatial configurations. In Canada, the dense urban cores of cities use less energy per person and produce lower levels of greenhouse gas emissions than the surrounding low-density suburbs. This is primarily because sustainable modes of transportation like transit, cycling, and walking are more heavily used in urban cores than they are in suburbs, which are dominated by automobiles. Additionally, low-density suburbs have higher water usage per person than urban cores due to the predominance of private gardens. And Canadian cities sprawling outwards into their surrounding hinterlands eat into prime farmlands.

Compact, dense urban forms are not a panacea, however, and can create environmental and social challenges as well. Buildings in cities are among the largest generators of direct greenhouse gas emissions and indirect emissions from electricity generation. The high-rise buildings that make up the dense urban areas of large Canadian cities are more energy-intensive per person than suburban homes, and produce significant greenhouse gas emissions due to requirements for elevators, lighting, and climate controls in common areas. Industrial activities in dense urban areas can produce harmful air, soil, and water pollutants with localized health impacts, as well as noise and land use conflicts with neighbours. Urban heat islands are another issue in built-up areas that lack sufficient greenspace and tree coverage. In Canadian cities, vulnerable populations are most likely to live in intensely developed locations where the heat island effect is especially pronounced.[4]

Beyond environmental issues directly related to urban form and buildings, the state of urban infrastructure also affects the sustainability of Canadian cities. Aging pipes are leading to considerable amounts of wasted water. Nonrenewable fossil fuels are still a leading source of power for many cities across the country, exacerbating the environmental impacts of the electricity used to power urban buildings and industrial activities. Programs to divert solid waste from landfills vary across the country, with wide discrepancies in the amount of garbage per capita being sidetracked to recycling and organic waste disposal facilities. And the lack of urban transit development has increased demand for property adjacent to existing transit stations, increasing property prices, catalyzing gentrification, and intensifying issues of unaffordability and unequal access to mobility.

Finally, urban policies, incentives, and pricing structures affect the sustainability of Canadian cities. Canadian cities often underprice or do not directly charge the full cost of public water, sewage, roads, and garbage disposal provision, leading to overconsumption that has negative environmental impact. In many municipalities, perverse incentives built into the zoning rules, design codes, building permitting process, and development charge regimes perpetuate sprawling development, or make it difficult to realize gentle urban intensification. And at a regional scale, land use and transportation planning is often carried out by separate departments within government, making it difficult to address mobility, housing, and affordability issues in a comprehensive, integrated manner.

Urban Environmental Policy Solutions

Canada's federalist governance system means that policies from all three levels of government must address the complex causes of urban environmental degradation. In recent years, city governments aggressively addressed environmental challenges in large measure because their impacts are very local. Moreover, Canadian cities are becoming testbeds for private sector firms developing environmental efficiency technologies.

Growth Management Policy

Given the critical role that urban form plays in a city's environmental sustainability, land-use policy is a key area that Canadian cities engage to address their environmental impact. In large cities across the country such as Vancouver, Toronto, Edmonton, and Calgary, similar regional growth-management strategies have been developed. The growth-management plans, drafted by both municipalities and provincial government departments, include provisions to protect natural environments, focus growth in compact, mixed-use communities, and provide rapid transit as a viable alternative to the automobile.

Despite the policy emphasis on compact development in transit-oriented communities, there are variations in the extent to which growth management strategies are aspirational or backed by enforceable rules, and the trend in Canadian cities continues to be towards urban spread and low-density development. Statistics Canada figures from 2016 show that infill development in core urban municipalities is being outpaced by growth in low-density peripheral municipalities. The fastest growing municipalities in the country are low density, auto-oriented suburbs around the periphery of major cities such as Cochrane and Airdrie in Calgary, Beaumont in Edmonton, and Milton in Greater Toronto. In these suburbs, housing with space and amenities for families costs less than in the urban core. This trend highlights a tension as growth-management planners work to provide affordable living space, services, and amenities that can accommodate a wide range of demographics, including families with children.

Green Policy

In addition to growth management plans, municipalities across Canada have developed a suite of urban sustainability and climate-change management plans. The aim of these plans is to improve the energy efficiency of existing buildings and transportation systems and reduce the greenhouse-gas intensity of energy sources by shifting towards renewable fuel sources, lower levels of waste production and disposal, and increase urban resilience to a changing climate.

As examples of the policy options being implemented, municipal district energy systems use alternative sources of energy to emit lower levels of emissions than conventional power plants and to improve reliability. Leading Canadian municipalities such as Toronto, Montreal, Vancouver, and Waterloo have mandated green roofs that can lower storm water runoff and reduce urban heat island effects. British Columbia and Quebec have permitted wood-framed midrise buildings of up to six stories under their building codes in order to lower development costs and improve housing affordability while supporting gentle land-use intensification. Soil treatment and recycling programs, such as those implemented by Waterfront Toronto, can reduce construction site waste. And green procurement policies can be integrated into government purchasing decisions to ensure that environmental protection is considered alongside value-for-money in government purchasing decisions.

Sustainable Transportation Policy

Canada is in the midst of the largest investment in sustainable urban transportation in a generation. Across the country, more subway, light rail, and bus rapid transit projects are being built than at any time in the last few decades. Importantly, these investments aim to provide new travel options and spur denser future developments in both dense urban cores and more auto-oriented suburbs. And they have been supported by dramatic increases in provincial and federal funding for capital investments in public transit that augment municipal spending. Municipalities such as Montreal and Vancouver have also expanded their cycling infrastructure, often through controversial projects that re-allocate road space to dedicated bicycle lanes. In order to reduce transportation emissions, municipal and provincial governments in Ontario and Quebec have electrified commuter rail networks and helped public and private vehicle fleets do the same. The environmental benefits of electrification depend greatly on how green underlying sources of electricity are in a given jurisdiction, which varies widely by province.

Over the past two decades, public transit's share of all commuting trips has increased only marginally in most of Canada's largest urban regions, offset by ongoing auto-dependence in the fast-growing outer suburbs. Governments do not always allocate scarce resources to the projects that will deliver the greatest environmental or societal benefit, posing a challenge to sustainability. The record on selecting transit projects based on the strength of the evidence as opposed to political considerations in Canada is decidedly mixed, and running rapid transit lines that are sited for political reasons and end up being under-utilized wastes scarce financial resources and does little to improve the urban environment.[5]

Private Sector Innovation

Private sector innovation is also enhancing the environmental sustainability of cities. Developers are experimenting with passive building designs, green building technologies, and modular construction technologies to lower energy usage, reduce building waste, and make housing more affordable. At the citywide scale, a wide range of "smart cities" technologies have emerged that can improve the environmental efficiency of cities, from censors embedded in roads to improve traffic flow to meters in parks that ensure that plants are only watered when needed. More disruptive innovations associated with the sharing economy in transportation and housing, as well as autonomous electric vehicles, are presented by their promoters as improving the environmental efficiency of cities, though these claims have been disputed. Nevertheless, Canadian municipal and provincial governments have passed regulations designed to make Canadian cities attractive test-beds for new green technologies and help them develop ecosystems of large and small firms that will drive the next generation of urban innovation.

Pricing

Finally, Canadian urban policymakers have used pricing policy to raise revenues to fund critical infrastructure and improve urban sustainability by influencing the level of user demand or spurring innovation to minimize the intensity of usage. In Canadian cities, water and electricity meters have been introduced so that residential customers can be charged for their individual usages rather than block rates. Parking fees on city streets have been increased. In Mississauga and Waterloo, residential stormwater charges have been introduced that vary depending on the estimated amount of hard surfaces on the property. And road charges have been implemented to fund infrastructure projects and maintain free-flowing traffic on a number of urban highways and bridges nationwide.

Yet the tensions between the environmental benefits of user fees as a way to moderate demand or incentivize the efficient use of scare resources, and the social and political dynamics of user fee implementation, are particularly pertinent in Canada. It has long been argued that high user fees on basic services like water, energy, and roads amount to a regressive tax that disproportionately impacts low-income users and can deter industrial employers who create jobs. User fees are also highly visible to the electorate and are often seen as politically unpopular. As a result, recent provincial and federal governments have taken high-profile steps to stop the introduction of tolls on highways such as the Don Valley Parkway and Gardiner Expressway in Toronto or the new Champlain Bridge in Montreal, or have removed tolls from existing facilities like the Port Mann and Golden Ears bridges in Vancouver. Furthermore, since 2017 the Ontario government has implemented measures to reduce electricity rates amidst widespread public outcry about rising energy costs. As such to date, despite the noted environmental benefits of charging user fees on services with negative environmental externalities, Canadian cities have not applied user fees as much as other international jurisdictions to encourage more efficient use of scarce resources.

Conclusions

In sum, cities must be a key focus for environmental policy in Canada. Cities are where the greatest amount of pollution is produced, and where interventions can have a significant impact because such a large share of the country's population live in cities. As illustrated above, to improve the environmental sustainability of cities, relevant authorities will need to combine land use and other green urban policies, enhancements in sustainable transportation, technological innovations, and public services pricing with negative environmental externalities that manage demand. However, in making themselves more sustainable, cities face barriers. First, some policies that address the environmental impacts of cities – such as higher prices on certain public services – can have implications on urban affordability, which is a major issue in Canada. One way government can solve this problem is by pledging the money generated from elevated user fees to provide alternative services that are more environmentally friendly and lower cost in communities directly impacted.

Second, the politics of urban policy means that the interventions that might deliver the greatest environmental benefits are not necessarily those that are most likely to be implemented. In Canada, highly visible mega-projects are often politically seductive, even when such initiatives are unlikely to deliver substantial environmental, user, or financial benefits. Indeed, to successfully leverage all of the recent policy interest and funding that has been dedicated to urban infrastructure and sustainability initiatives in Canada, it is critical that evidence-based decision making be a core policy principle. Otherwise, future Canadians may look back at the current moment as a missed opportunity.

NOTES

1 Statistics Canada, "Canada Goes Urban," *The Daily*, April 20, 2015, https://www150.statcan.gc.ca/n1/pub/11-630-x/11-630-x2015004-eng. htm.
2 "Climate Change – UN-Habitat," accessed June 29, 2018, https:// unhabitat.org/urban-themes/climate-change/.
3 Christopher A. Kennedy, Iain Stewart, Angelo Facchini, Igor Cersosimo, Renata Mele, Bin Chen, Mariko Uda, et al., "Energy and Material Flows of Megacities," *Proceedings of the National Academy of Sciences* 112, no. 19 (May 12, 2015): 5985.
4 See Kate Allen, "Reducing Urban Heat Island Effect in Toronto a Matter of Social Justice, Experts Say," *Toronto Star*, August 17, 2013, https://www. thestar.com/news/world/2013/08/17/reducing_urban_heat_island_ effect_in_toronto_a_matter_of_social_justice_activists_say.html.
5 Shoshanna Saxe, Eric Miller, and Peter Guthrie, "The Net Greenhouse Gas Impact of the Sheppard Subway Line," *Transportation Research Part D: Transport and Environment* 51 (March 1, 2017): 261–75.

10 Canada's Radical Fiscal Federation: The Next Fifty Years[1]

KEVIN MILLIGAN

Canadians have created a radical fiscal federation. According to 2014 data compiled by the OECD, 78 per cent of spending in Canada happens at subnational levels of government. In the United States, it's 48 per cent. Across the OECD, the average is just 32 per cent.[2] Canada is a radical outlier.

In this essay, I start by exploring how we have become fiscally radical. I introduce and dismiss three possible explanations for the source of our status as a fiscal outlier: our constitution, our arguably weak sense of national common purpose, and our systems of political accountability. I then argue that economic efficiency is the source of our radical fiscal federation. Last, I consider how our fiscal federation should evolve to meet the principal fiscal challenge for the next fifty years: rising provincial health expenditures.

How is it that Canada alone among OECD countries can maintain a modern welfare state mostly run by provinces, some with only a few hundred thousand people? How can we raise the taxes to do so? There are several usual answers to these questions, but they provide incomplete and unsatisfactory explanations.

Is it our constitution? Sections 92 and 93 of the 1867 British North America Act assigned responsibility for hospitals, schools, and education to the provinces. Moreover, public insurance funds (such as for unemployment) were considered provincial jurisdiction under the "property and civil rights" heading of Section 92.[3] This constitutional division of powers set the initial conditions, but it insufficiently explains Canada's current radical decentralization. It is hard to argue that constitutional divisions of power have provided an insuperable impediment to centralization, as economic forces have frequently overcome those original constitutional allocations through amendments to the constitution.[4] So, constitutional forces alone cannot account for Canada's decentralization.

Is it Canada's people? Does Canada lack a sense of nation strong enough to drive national economic integration?[5] Many other developed nation-states similar to Canada are also cobbled together from historically independent and culturally diverse regions: Germany, Spain, Italy, Switzerland, and Belgium, to name a few. To explain Canada's radical federation, one needs to argue that Canada lacks national solidarity compared to these other countries. As one example, Belgium is a country with very distinct cultural and linguistic groups, yet the Belgian central government has a spending share twice that of Canada's.

What about fiscal accountability? There are vast disparities between what provincial governments spend and what they raise in taxes. Prince Edward Island gets 38 per cent of its total revenue from federal transfers. For Nova Scotia and New Brunswick, the share is 35 per cent. For B.C. it is 18 per cent. Such mismatches generate concern about political accountability: voters properly monitor spending and taxation that occurs at different levels of government?[6] Have we developed some unique formula of political accountability that allows us to get away with these vast fiscal disparities when other OECD countries can't? This seems unlikely.

Economic Roots of Radical Decentralization

So far, I've argued that the radical position of Canada's fiscal federation can't easily be explained by constitutional constraints, weak national ties, or overachieving models of fiscal accountability. I now proceed to what I see as the source of Canada's difference: we have found a way to organize our federal and provincial fiscal affairs efficiently.[7] There are two main roots of this efficiency: intergovernmental transfers and centralized tax administration through tax collection agreements.

Intergovernmental transfers have constitutional origins, and are certainly held aloft by national sentiments. But the strongest argument for our transfer system is economic efficiency. The scope and scale for efficient production of government-provided goods varies. For some goods, like education or parks, local or provincial governments can manage the spending efficiently. For others, like transportation or environment, a national or even global viewpoint is necessary to provide government services efficiently. That is the spending side. But the same is true as well for the efficiency of taxation, owing to the mobility or immobility of different tax bases. Sales and consumption taxes can vary across local jurisdictions without much economic cost, while at the other end, corporate and capital income is much more mobile and so might best be handled centrally.

Imagine if both taxes and spending were assigned to the optimal level of government, taking only efficiency into account. Economist Albert Breton noticed fifty years ago that it would be a great coincidence if optimal spending and tax assignment resulted in balanced budgets at each level of government.[8] So, intergovernmental grants are required to maintain economic efficiency; if we didn't have a strong system of intergovernmental grants, either spending or taxation in Canada would be set inefficiently.

The second main factor is our system of tax collection agreements. For GST/HST, corporate, and personal taxes, most provinces allow the federal government to collect taxes on their behalf.[9] The provinces have scope to choose rates and some exemptions, but it is the federal government that does the actual collection at source and the administration. The provinces just have to cash the cheques they receive from Ottawa.

This arrangement allows decentralized decisions about the level and type of taxes. It aligns spending with taxes to the degree possible, which bolsters fiscal accountability. It saves taxpayers money by creating a national economic space with comparable rules and administration, rather than a complex balkanized system. It also saves money by avoiding the replication of a separate tax administration apparatus in every province and territory.

So, why has Canada been able to radically decentralize the fiscal operations of its federation more than any other OECD country? We have figured out economically efficient ways to do so that other countries have not yet followed. That's where Canada is now, in the sesquicentennial year.

Trouble Ahead

Where will the Canadian fiscal federation be fifty years from now, in the bicentennial year of 2067? The Parliamentary Budget Officer produces an annual projection of fiscal sustainability for the federal and provincial governments. Figure 10.1 shows the projected path of the debt-to-GDP ratio over the next fifty years for both provincial and federal governments. The federal government, on its current trajectory,

Figure 10.1. Canada's Debt-to-GDP Ratio, 2017–2067[10]

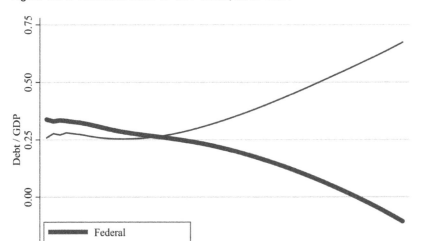

will fully pay off its net debt by 2060. Program spending and transfers to children, the unemployed, and the elderly are not projected to be long-run challenges. Old age pensions for the baby boomer generation hit their peak in 2031 and decline thereafter. The federal government is in a sustainable long-run fiscal position. The provinces, on the other hand, are not in a sustainable fiscal position. According to these projections, debt begins increasing in the mid-2020s and follows an explosive path. The reason is health care spending.

For at least two decades economists have warned that health costs would rise substantially in the future, but up to now this prediction has had mixed results.[11] After rapid cost increases in the first decade of the 2000s, the Canadian Institute for Health Information reports that the annual real increase over the five years from 2010–2014 was negative 0.2 per cent.[12]

But demographic pressures are only now starting to accelerate. Health spending rises substantially at older ages – especially after age 75. The share of the population over age 75 will start to rise in the 2020s and by the 2040s will be double the current share.[13] These demographic realities are fixed into our population structure and unlikely to surprise.

While the provinces' successes in controlling costs over the last decade should give pause to any economist making predictions, it is clear that population aging will demand a sharp quickening in the pace of cost innovation.

In my view, the most likely outcome is provincial budgets will be increasingly strained through the 2020s. To get a sense of the magnitudes, take the case of British Columbia. The C.D. Howe Institute projects health spending will increase by three percentage points of GDP by 2030 – just a few years from now.[14] That level of spending would require approximately a doubling of either the provincial income tax or sales tax. Those are substantial tax increases in just a dozen years from now.

A Framework

To build solutions for Canada's upcoming fiscal challenges, I lay out a framework for analysis based on the work of economists Richard Musgrave and Wallace Oates. In his classic public finance textbook, Richard Musgrave considered the economic underpinnings of federations, and how taxes ought to be assigned to different levels of government.[15] The key consideration for efficiency is the mobility of the tax base. I argued earlier that the sales tax base can be handled efficiently locally, while corporate taxes are more mobile and better handled centrally.

To make progress, we need to add Wallace Oates's fiscal federalism approach to the framework.[16] Oates argues that central governments are good at things requiring coordination across subnational boundaries – when decisions in one place affect people in other places. But Oates also recognizes the advantages of subnational governments, which can account for local circumstances more adroitly than a faraway central government. So, the Oates model rests on a tension between these two factors. Central governments are better at coordinating when decisions in one place affect people in other places, but subnational governments can account for local circumstances.

In recent work with Michael Smart, I combine the frameworks of Musgrave and Oates to reconsider tax assignment in a federation, with particular attention paid to personal income taxation.[17] We start with the Musgrave argument – that mobile factors are likely best taxed centrally. We then add an Oatesian perspective. Since provinces have vastly different income distributions, it seems efficient to have different taxation of high-income people in different provinces. Our theoretical model grapples with this trade-off. Central government income taxation can limit cross-province income shifting while provincial income taxation can address local situations. We find that the best way forward is for the federal and provincial governments to share responsibility for income taxation.

This economic framework delivers clear guidance on how we might assign taxation efficiently in our Canadian federation. Both the mobility of factors and the differences in circumstance across provinces need to be considered in any solution.

Radical Solutions

I consider three policy options. The first is a status quo option that leaves provinces on their own to raise substantial new funds as health costs accelerate. But, the provinces where the aging problems are most acute – places like Nova Scotia and New Brunswick – already have the highest personal taxes, the highest corporate taxes, and the highest sales taxes. How can these provinces raise substantially more revenue – on the order of 3 or 4 per cent of GDP just fifteen years from now – in a federation with mobile factors? Relying on a scaled-up version of the existing tax structure would be difficult.

The next option is to federalize the coming health costs by raising the money in Ottawa and sending higher transfers to the provinces. This option would certainly require a major change in the level of federal taxes. By the late 2030s, we'd need something on the order of six more points on the federal part of GST/HST or a 40 per cent increase of federal personal income taxes. The main challenge to this approach is fiscal accountability; a mismatch between who raises and who spends money. Will provincial governments be as attentive to health cost decisions if Ottawa is paying the bill?

A third option is to radically reorder our tax assignment between the federal and provincial governments, guided by efficiency as laid out in the framework. Currently, provincial governments raise about CDN $26 billion in corporate taxes. Corporate income is relatively mobile.[18] This revenue could be swapped to the federal government in exchange for GST/HST tax room to the provinces. On an approximately revenue neutral basis, this swap would cost four out of the five current federal GST/HST points. Then, as funding needs grow in the decades to come, provinces can raise their GST/HST rates as required. The final piece of this proposal is the maintenance of a robust and strong equalization grant, so that provinces without large resource revenues can maintain their relative position within the federation.[19]

I therefore propose a three-part plan. One, provinces vacate corporate taxation. Two, the federal government vacates the GST/HST space – but continues its efficient central collection through the Canada Revenue Agency. Three, Ottawa maintains a robust equalization grant. This plan has several advantages. A tax assignment based on the Musgrave principle of tax base mobility bring efficiency gains, but provinces retain tools sufficient to adjust both for revenue and fairness. The current efficient administration is maintained, with tax collection agreements facilitating common structure but provincial rate-setting. Fiscal accountability is ensured, as a province paying insufficient attention to innovation in the efficient delivery of health services will be punished by voters facing higher provincial GST/HST rates. Finally, corporate income tax is a very volatile source whereas sales tax is much more stable. Health spending does not vary substantially through the business cycle, so it makes sense to match health spending with a stable financing source.

Of course, this reform would not be easy. While the revenue implications of swapping corporate taxes for GST/HST might be made to balance overall, some provinces might gain and others lose in such a swap. On precedent, Quebec may refuse to participate in such a swap. Finally, provinces facing a particularly large increase in the elderly population share may still find it difficult to raise their GST/HST rates substantially over other provinces' rates.

Conclusion

By international standards, Canada's fiscal federation is radically decentralized. I argue here that the institutions that have evolved to facilitate this decentralization – intergovernmental transfers and centralized tax administration – are sustained by economic efficiency. The fiscal federation will face steep challenges in the next few decades as provincial health spending strains the existing arrangements. Radical solutions may therefore be required to maintain a decentralized federation. A swap of corporate taxation to the federal government in exchange for provincial control over substantially all sales tax revenue would improve the efficiency of our tax system as it prepares to meet the needs of the next fifty years of confederation.

NOTES

1 This paper was prepared for the conference "Canada and its Centennial and Sesquicentennial" held at the University of Toronto in November 2017. A version of this work was presented as the Graham Lecture at Dalhousie University in November, 2017. The author thanks conference participants and Graham Lecture attendees for feedback and suggestions that were incorporated into this chapter.
2 OECD, *OECD Regions at a Glance 2016*, 2016, https://www.oecd-ilibrary.org/content/publication/reg_glance-2016-en.
3 Supreme Court of Canada Reference re legislative jurisdiction of Parliament of Canada to enact the Employment and Social Insurance Act (1935, c. 48), [1936] S.C.R. 427.
4 Constitutional amendments to facilitate federal spending on social programs occurred in 1940 (unemployment insurance), 1951 (Old Age Security), and 1964 (Canada Pension Plan).
5 See the discussion of "sharing communities" in Keith Banting and Robin Boadway, "Defining the Sharing Community: The Federal Role in Health Care," in *Money, Politics and Health Care*, ed. Harvey Lazar and France St-Hilaire (Montreal: Institute for Research on Public Policy, 2004), 1–77.
6 For Canadian evidence and discussion of political accountability in a federation, see Fred Cutler, "Government Responsibility and Electoral Accountability in Federations," *Publius: The Journal of Federalism* 34, no. 2 (January 1, 2004): 19–38; Fred Cutler, "Whodunnit? Voters and Responsibility in Canadian Federalism," *Canadian Journal of Political Science/Revue Canadienne de Science Politique* 41, no. 3 (September 2008): 627–54.
7 The arguments in this section resonate with Heath, who argues that most government spending in Canada can be motivated by efficiency considerations rather than purely as redistributive. See Joseph Heath, *The Efficient Society: Why Canada Is as Close to Utopia as It Gets* (Toronto: Penguin Canada, 2001).
8 See Albert Breton, "A Theory of Government Grants," *Canadian Journal of Economics and Political Science* 31, no. 2 (May 1965): 175–87.
9 In this essay I use "GST/HST" to refer to the Goods and Services Tax and Harmonized Sales Tax system, with a federal component everywhere and a provincial component in most provinces.
10 The most recent edition was published as "Fiscal Sustainability Report 2017," Parliamentary Budget Officer, accessed April 12, 2018, http://www.pbo-dpb.gc.ca/en/blog/news/FSR_October_2017.

11 For the demographic case for concern about health spending, see Frank
    T. Denton and Byron G. Spencer, "Demographic Change and the Cost
    of Publicly Funded Health Care," *Canadian Journal on Aging* 14, no. 2
    (January 1995): 174–92; William B.P. Robson, "Time and Money: The Chal-
    lenge of Demographic Change and Government Finances in Canada," *C.D.
    Howe Institute*, Backgrounder, no. 109 (December 2007): 1–11; David A.
    Dodge and Richard Dion, "Chronic Healthcare Spending Disease: A Macro
    Diagnosis and Prognosis," *C.D. Howe Institute*, Commentary, no. 317
    (April 6, 2011): 1–16; or J.C. Herbert Emery, David Still, and Thomas J.
    Cottrell, "Can We Avoid a Sick Fiscal Future? The Non-Sustainability of
    Health-Care Spending with an Aging Population," SPP Research Paper, no.
    12–31 (October 17, 2012). For an argument against the demographic con-
    cerns, see Robert G. Evans, Kimberlyn M. McGrail, Steven G. Morgan,
    Morris L. Barer, and Clyde Hertzman, "APOCALYPSE NO: Population
    Aging and The Future of Health Care Systems," *Canadian Journal on Aging*
    20, no. S1 (summer 2001): 160–91. For the argument that technology-driven
    innovation can combat the demographic challenge, see Will Falk, Matthew
    Mendelsohn, and Josh Hjartarson, "Fiscal Sustainability and the Transforma-
    tion of Canada's Healthcare System," Mowat Centre Shifting Gears Report,
    2011, https://mowatcentre.ca/fiscal-sustainability-canadas-healthcare/.
12 See Canadian Institute for Health Information (https://www.cihi.ca/en)
    for the most recent release of national health expenditure data.
13 Data taken from CANSIM table 052-0005, medium growth projection
    scenario.
14 For demographic-based projections for British Columbia, see William B.P.
    Robson, Colin Busby, and Aaron Jacobs, "Healthcare and an Aging Popu-
    lation: Managing Slow-Growing Revenues and Rising Health Spending in
    British Columbia," *C.D. Howe Institute Ebrief* 195 (December 17, 2014).
15 Richard A. Musgrave, *The Theory of Public Finance: A Study in Public Econ-
    omy* (New York: McGraw-Hill, 1959).
16 Wallace E. Oates, *Fiscal Federalism* (New York: Harcourt Brace Jovanovich,
    1972).
17 See Kevin Milligan and Michael Smart, "An estimable model of income
    redistribution in a federation: Musgrave meets Oates," forthcoming in
    American Economic Journal: Economic Policy.
18 For evidence on cross province corporate income shifting, see Jack Mintz
    and Michael Smart, "Income Shifting, Investment, and Tax Competition:
    Theory and Evidence from Provincial Taxation in Canada," *Journal of Public
    Economics* 88, no. 6 (June 1, 2004): 1149–68. They find very high elasticities
    of corporate income when provincial corporate tax rates change.

19 There is a long history in Canada of re-examining tax assignment in the federation, going back to the Rowell-Sirois Commission and the Royal Commission on Taxation (Carter Commission). Reorganizing corporate taxes at the federal level is not a new proposal; for an example, see Irene K. Ip and Jack M. Mintz, with a commentary by Claude E. Forget, "Dividing the Spoils: The Federal-Provincial Allocation of Taxing Powers," *The Canada Round* 11, C.D. Howe Institute, 1992. For a review of the literature, see Richard M. Bird and Jack M. Mintz, "Tax Assignment in Canada: A Modest Proposal," in *Toward a New Mission Statement For Canadian Fiscal Federalism*, ed. Harvey Lazar (Montreal: McGill-Queen's University Press, 2000), 263–92.

PART THREE

Rethinking Sovereignty, Allegiance, and Rights

11 Reasonable Accommodation, Diversity, and the Supreme Court of Canada

EMMETT MACFARLANE

Canada's centennial marked a time when the country began to recognize its increasing diversity through formal public policy. The establishment of official languages policy in 1969 and multiculturalism policy in 1971 reflected values later entrenched in our constitutional order, principally via the *Charter of Rights and Freedoms*, alongside related provisions like equality rights and freedom of religion. Constitutional entrenchment of these values, however, is not alone a sufficient condition for resolving problems and tensions relating to diversity in Canada. The 2017 enactment of Bill 62 in Quebec, banning face coverings for public sector workers and for anyone using public services (such as taking the bus or going to a hospital), is only the most recent example of problematic public policy that flies in the face of constitutionally protected values. The law, whose title begins "An Act to foster adherence to State religious neutrality ...," specifically targets the niqab.

As Canada celebrates its sesquicentennial, this chapter explores the role constitutional rights play in accommodating diversity under multiculturalism. Specifically, how good of a job does the Supreme Court do in addressing policy disputes relating to values like multiculturalism? To do full justice to this question would require exploring a comprehensive list of cases not only relating to equality rights and freedom of religion, but other rights that may come into conflict with multicultural values. In lieu of that and in the limited space available, this chapter focuses on a subset of cases specifically implicating reasonable accommodation. These cases typically involve limits placed on religious minorities through policies with objectives ranging from identification or security concerns to contexts where the rights of others may be at stake. While the Court has a relatively coherent approach to religious freedom claims, it has struggled with the very question of reasonable limits on those rights. I briefly conclude by noting that the Court's composition – there has never been a person of colour appointed to the bench – may negatively impact the symbolic legitimacy of its jurisprudence in cases involving diversity. Further, there is some evidence from the study of judicial behaviour that modes of representation are more than symbolic and can actually influence decision-making in the Court. In this sense, the Court's influence on policies implicating diversity could itself be informed by the relative lack of diversity on the bench.

Diversity and Challenges of Jurisprudence

Few of the notable equality rights cases that have been heard by the Supreme Court since 1982 have involved reasonable accommodation or multiculturalism policy. While there have been significant section 15 cases implicating the rights of women[1] and gays and lesbians,[2] reasonable accommodation cases have almost exclusively rested on freedom of religion. The Court has notoriously struggled with the equality rights section of the Charter, which recently-retired Chief Justice Beverley McLachlin has famously called "the most difficult right."[3] The Court's justices have consistently disagreed on a reliable approach to identifying discrimination. In 1999, for example, the Court introduced the concept of "human dignity" into its analysis, only to abandon it a decade later after relevant interest groups complained that requiring the impairment of someone's human dignity as a factor for recognizing discrimination meant that it was too difficult for equality rights claimants to succeed.[4]

Critics of the Court's approach to Section 15 of the Charter have argued that it has not sufficiently dealt with systemic discrimination and that it has at times avoided dealing with equality rights altogether.[5] There is some truth to this: in cases with important implications for the rights of women or the rights of people with disabilities – including cases relating to abortion,[6] prostitution,[7] medical aid in dying,[8] and supervised drug injection[9] – the Court has resorted to Section 7's right to life, liberty, and security of the person, a legal right, instead of assessing the policies in light of equality rights. By doing so, the Court misses an opportunity to get policymakers to think about policies that may have a discriminatory impact on disadvantaged groups and to approach policy from an explicitly equality rights-enhancing perspective.

Section 27, the "interpretative clause" on multiculturalism, similarly represents a missed opportunity from a jurisprudential perspective. The term "multiculturalism" appears in 47 Supreme Court Charter decisions, but in only a handful does Section 27 play any major role. Section 27 states that the Charter "shall be interpreted in a manner consistent with the preservation and enhancement of the multicultural heritage of Canadians." In the 1990 *Keegstra* case on hate speech, for example, the justices ruled that Section 27 should not be used to interpret the scope of freedom of expression, but rather become relevant at the "reasonable limits" stage of analysis.[10] In that case, the Court specifically emphasized the value of multiculturalism as a constitutional principle that supports Parliament's objective of limiting hate speech. Two decades later, the Court makes no mention of multiculturalism or Section 27 in its analysis of the most recent significant case involving hate speech.[11]

Religious Freedom and Reasonable Accommodation

Freedom of religion, which is implicated in many reasonable accommodation controversies, is a bit of a different story. In contrast to the disagreement over equality rights, the Court has generally agreed on a basic definition of – and, more recently, an approach to – religious freedom. In an early case, the Court declared that the purpose of freedom of conscience and religion is to ensure

> that every individual be free to hold and to manifest whatever beliefs and opinions his or her conscience dictates, provided *inter alia* only that such manifestations do not injure his or her neighbors or their parallel rights to hold and manifest beliefs and opinions of their own.[12]

In the 2004 *Syndicat Northcrest* case, the Court noted that rights claimants "should not need to prove the objective validity of their beliefs in that their beliefs are objectively recognized as valid by other members of the same religion."[13] As a result, the Court has taken the position that freedom of religion includes the freedom to hold and manifest beliefs, so long as the claimant holds a *sincere belief* that a particular practice is required by his or her religion. This principle ensures that the Court can avoid engaging in theology and questions about religious requirements.

This approach is precisely why bans on the niqab need to be justified as a limit on a right: where some people may assert that the niqab is not a religious requirement under Islam, what matters is whether the rights claimant holds a sincere belief that it is one. Yet despite this basic agreement on an approach, the justices have frequently disagreed about whether certain policies imposed reasonable limits on religious accommodation. In *Syndicat Northcrest*, the Court split 5 to 4 on whether Orthodox Jews could set up succahs on the balconies of their apartments, finding for the claimants. In *Hutterian Brethren*, the Court split 4 to 3 in upholding a provincial law requiring the use of photos for driver's licenses.[14] And in *R. v. NS* the Court split three ways over the issue of whether a sexual assault complainant would be required to remove her niqab while testifying at trial.[15]

One of the things these divided cases tell us is that the Court has had some trouble weighing the balance between government policy objectives and minority rights. While the division in *NS* might be understandable due to the difficult quagmire regarding how the complainant's religious freedom to wear her niqab might impact the accused's right to a fair trial, the other two cases pose no such competing rights claims. In *Syndicat Northcrest*, three justices dissented on the basis that, given that the sincere beliefs of the claimants would entertain alternatives to a personal succah, another form of accommodation was possible (though a fourth judge dissented to uphold the ban on the basis of the competing rights of the other co-owners to enjoy their property). In *Hutterian Brethren*, the majority upheld the law on the basis that the government's objective in maintaining the driver's license system and preventing identity theft was sufficiently important. The dissenting justices held that the government did not sufficiently justify the infringement, particularly given that religious exemptions had previously been granted for twenty-nine years under the law and the lack of evidence that identity theft had been a concern.

It remains an open question whether the sort of proportionality analysis the courts engage in under the Charter's reasonable limits assessment is clear enough to deal with the tough balancing act called for in many reasonable accommodation cases. The Court was able to reach a unanimous decision in favour of nullifying a school board's decision banning a Sikh student from wearing his kirpan (a ceremonial blunted dagger) to school.[16] It is not clear why similar consensus could not be reached in the other cases described above.

Despite this, the Court's stated approach to religious freedom makes it clear that Quebec's Bill 62 is unlikely to survive constitutional challenge. Although the government has defended the law on a range of grounds, including state religious neutrality, security, and the need to identify people, it is unlikely these objectives will meet constitutional muster. There is little evidence that security or identification concerns meet a "pressing and substantial" objective in the context of accessing public services like transit. And the primary justification, state neutrality in religion, is a symbolic objective, something the courts are unlikely to uphold in the face of an obvious Charter violation.

Yet there is also recent evidence that the Court's approach to defining freedom of religion is not as straightforward as it seems. A 2017 case arguably suggests that the Court has a narrowly Eurocentric view of religious freedom, as it ruled in favour of the development of a ski resort despite arguments that doing so would impair the religious beliefs and practices of members of the Ktunaxa Nation.[17] The claimants asserted that the project would drive the Grizzly Bear Spirit from an area they call Qat'muk. The majority ruled that the claim falls outside the scope of religious freedom, which has two aspects: "the freedom to hold religious beliefs and the freedom to manifest those beliefs."[18] The majority asserted that the "state's duty under s. 2(a) is not to protect the object of beliefs, such as Grizzly Bear Spirit. Rather, the state's duty is to protect everyone's freedom to hold such beliefs and to manifest them in worship and practice or by teaching and dissemination. In short, the Charter protects the freedom to worship, but does not protect the spiritual focal point of worship."[19] By contrast, two judges in a concurring opinion disagreed, arguing that the state rendered the claimants' "sincerely held religious beliefs devoid of all religious significance" and thus constituted an infringement. However, they also determined that the government's decision to approve the development was proportionate, in that it balanced the rights at stake with relevant government objectives, and so ruled with the majority in the result.[20]

Diversity of the Court

The Ktunaxa Nation decision raises a difficult question of whether the Court is guilty of refusing to interpret the rights of minority groups in a manner consistent with how those groups conceive of rights. This in turn raises a representational concern. There are well established "democratic" objections to judicial review and the power of courts to influence public policy.[21] Yet as it relates to the protection of minority rights in some of these cases, the problem with giving courts the final say over the policies at stake is not that we have unelected judges overruling elected majorities, but that judges, knowing they have the final say, are often deferential to government policy objectives in the precise context that they should be the prototypical defenders of minority rights.[22] Deference may be called for in many Charter cases, but when the state is acting as the "singular antagonist" of minority rights,[23] where other peoples' rights are not equally implicated, courts need to draw clearer and brighter lines around the constitutionality of particular policies.

One important potential factor is the fact the Court itself has been a laggard when it comes to diversity. As noted above, there has never been a non-white judge appointed to the bench. In scholarly studies of judicial behaviour, we know that women judges decide differently than men.[24] For example, women judges have been found to be 27 per cent more likely than men to rule in favour of discrimination claimants in equality rights cases and 54 per cent more likely to do so in non-unanimous cases.[25] It should not be a surprise that women have brought an experiential perspective to the law, and there is good reason to think that Indigenous or other minority perspectives would as well.

This is not to suggest that there are homogeneous identity-based views, or that judges "speak for" their sex or racial or ethnic groups. Nor is it to suggest that the new perspectives brought into an increasingly diverse bench ought to necessarily win the day. Yet the Court suffers symbolically, and likely substantively, from its relative lack of representational diversity. The Court's jurisprudence, particularly on rights issues implicating diversity, can only be sharpened by bringing new forms of experiential wisdom to the bench.

NOTES

1 *Symes v. Canada*, [1993] 4 S.C.R. 695; *Thibaudeau v. Canada*, [1995] 2 S.C.R. 627; *Newfoundland (Treasury Board) v. N.A.P.E.*, [2004] 3 S.C.R. 381, 2004 SCC 66.

2 *Egan v. Canada*, [1995] 2 S.C.R. 513; *Vriend v. Alberta*, [1998] 1 S.C.R. 493; *M. v. H.*, [1999] 2 S.C.R.; *Reference re Same-Sex Marriage*, [2004] 3 S.C.R. 698, 2004 SCC 79.

3 The Right Honourable Beverley McLachlin, "Equality: The Most Difficult Right," *Supreme Court Law Review* 14, Ar. 2 (2001): 17, 19.

4 *Law v. Canada (Minister of Employment and Immigration)*, [1999] 1 S.C.R. 497; *R. v. Kapp*, [2008] 2 S.C.R. 483, 2008 SCC 41.

5 See, for example, Jonnette Watson Hamilton and Jennifer Koshan, "Adverse Impact: The Supreme Court's Approach to Adverse Effects Discrimination under Section 15 of the Charter," *Review of Constitutional Studies* 19 (2015 2014): 191–236; Emmett Macfarlane, "Dialogue, Remedies, and Positive Rights: *Carter v. Canada* as Microcosm for Past and Future Issues under the Charter of Rights and Freedoms," *Ottawa Law Review* 49, no. 1 (2017): 107–29.

6 *R. v. Morgentaler*, [1988] 1 S.C.R. 30.

7 *Canada (Attorney General) v. Bedford*, 2013 SCC 72, [2013] 3 S.C.R. 1101.

8 *Carter v. Canada (Attorney General)*, 2015 SCC 5, [2015] 1 S.C.R. 331.

9 *Canada (Attorney General) v. PHS Community Services Society*, 2011 SCC 44, [2011] 3 S.C.R. 134.

10 *R. v. Keegstra*, [1990] 3 S.C.R. 697.

11 *Saskatchewan (Human Rights Commission) v. Whatcott*, 2013 SCC 11, [2013] 1 S.C.R. 467.

12 *R. v. Big M Drug Mart Ltd.*, [1985] 1 S.C.R. 295 at para. 123.

13 *Syndicat Northcrest v. Amselem*, [2004] 2 S.C.R. 551, 2004 SCC 47.

14 *Alberta v. Hutterian Brethren of Wilson Colony*, 2009 SCC 37, [2009] 2 S.C.R. 567.

15 *R. v. N.S.*, 2012 SCC 72, [2012] 3 S.C.R. 726.

16 *Multani v. Commission scolaire Marguerite-Bourgeoys*, [2006] 1 S.C.R. 256, 2006 SCC 6.

17 *Ktunaxa Nation v. British Columbia (Forests, Lands and Natural Resource Operations)*, 2017 SCC 54.

18 *Ibid* at para. 63.

19 *Ibid* at para. 71.

20 *Ibid* at paras. 118–19.

21 Jeremy Waldron, "The Core of the Case against Judicial Review Essay," *Yale Law Journal* 115 (2006 2005): 1346–407; F.L. Morton and Rainer Knopff, *The Charter Revolution and the Court Party* (Peterborough, ON: Broadview Press, 2000).

22 The idea that courts are generally deferential to the dominant governing coalition is a central tenet of the regime politics thesis. See Emmett Macfarlane, "'You Can't Always Get What You Want': Regime Politics, the Supreme Court of Canada, and the Harper Government," *Canadian Journal of Political Science* 51, no. 1 (March 2018): 1–21.

23 *Irwin Toy Ltd. v. Quebec (Attorney General)*, [1989] 1 S.C.R. 927.

24 Emmett Macfarlane, *Governing from the Bench: The Supreme Court of Canada and the Judicial Role* (Vancouver: UBC Press, 2013): 63–4.

25 C.L. Ostberg and Matthew Wetstein, *Attitudinal Decision Making in the Supreme Court of Canada* (Vancouver: UBC Press, 2007): 134–9.

12 Invisibility, Wilful Blindness, and Impending Doom: The Future (if Any) of Canadian Federalism[1]

JEAN LECLAIR

"... Canada's constitutional law can be likened to a verb. It sustains, negates, inflects, modifies, or transforms relationships and states of being. Like a verb, Canada's constitution located us in time – with a past, present and future tense. It explains what brought us together, and what should happen now and later on to sustain our togetherness and measured separateness. Thus, like a verb, Canada's constitution regulates relationships through time; it links objects (persons, places and things) to a reciprocal series of obligations in the real world."

John Borrows[2]

"[N]ous devons rester optimistes parce que courir à la catastrophe est le lot de toutes les espèces, parce que la catastrophe est un mode d'évolution normal que ce soit pour les plantes, les animaux ou les êtres humains. Nous faisons partie du monde vivant, nous courons donc naturellement à la catastrophe."

Boris Cyrulnik[3]

I never thought of Winston S. Churchill as a political theorist. However, at the very beginning of his *Memoirs of the Second World War*, he states the following:

It is my purpose, as one who lived and acted in these days, to show how easily the tragedy of the Second World War could have been prevented; how the malice of the wicked was reinforced by the weakness of the virtuous; how the structure and habits of democratic states, unless they are welded together into larger organisms, lack those elements of persistence and conviction which can alone give security to humble masses; how, even in matters of self-preservation, no policy is pursued even for ten or fifteen years at a time. We shall see how the counsels of prudence and restraint may become the prime agents of mortal danger; how the middle course adopted from desires for safety and a quiet life may be found to lead direct to the bull's-eye of disaster.[4]

I believe, as David Suzuki does, that "the survival of humans as a species depends on what we [will] do in the next few years," and that failure to act will lead to our extinction before the end of this century.[5] We are thus in the midst of the most dramatic period of not just Canadian history, but human history. And, along with Churchill, I am not quite certain whether our present liberal-democratic political structures will be capable of withstanding the telluric turbulences engendered by the draconian measures plain survival will necessarily call for.

With that in mind I will address the question whether Canadian federalism is fit to meet the challenges of the future. I will try to demonstrate that part of our plight has to do with the way we conceive law, and more precisely how we apprehend constitutions, constitutionalism, and federalism.

I will claim that by equating law with inanimate abstract norms, by conceiving the concept of law as a noun rather than a as verb[6] – that is, as a hierarchy of rules rather than, in the words of Lon L. Fuller, "a complex syste[m] of order that came into existence, not by a single act of creation, but through the cumulative effect of countless purposive directions of human effort"[7] – we fail to grasp the relational character of law and constitutional law. By doing so, we lose sight of the human interactions hidden under the veil of notions such as "autonomy and rights," "aboriginal title," "sovereignty," "peoples," and "nation," etc.

Most importantly, our conceptualizations have made invisible two profoundly important Canadian constituent actors: the nonhuman natural world and future generations. Our survival will depend on our ability to admit the complex relationships we, as Canadians, entertain with these living and yet unborn entities, and our ability to acknowledge their existence in the legal and constitutional fora.

Hiding Law's Relational Dimension

As any other discipline, law proceeds by way of conceptualizations that inevitably reify the reality they seek to describe.[8] "Autonomy" and "Rights," "aboriginal title," "sovereignties," "peoples," and "nations" have never been directly seen or heard; no one has ever shared coffee or wine with any of them. They are social constructions, concepts we use to make sense of our world, and which, for the most part, have no true existence outside of our common imagination. Be that as it may, these notions most certainly shape our behaviours.

These concepts and the rules they authorize are certainly enabling, but oftentimes disabling. Because they are approached as nouns, the tendency is to try to decipher their ontological characteristics in the abstract. In so doing, law's discourse acquires an impersonality that hides its fundamentally relational character and its deep anchoring in human interactions.

For instance, autonomy and rights are not simply about barriers and boundaries; they are proxies for determining how human interactions can be channelled in ways that "can develop and sustain both an enriching collective life and [provide] scope for genuine individual autonomy."[9] Aboriginal title refers to the complex web of relationships between Indigenous and non-Indigenous peoples and governments exercising agency over a particular territory. Sovereignty or political power "is generated from the particular relationship that evolves between the sovereign and subject, government and citizens."[10]

This same tendency to approach legal constructs from an abstract perspective affects our understanding of constitutions, constitutionalism, and federalism by hiding from view their essentially dynamic dimension.

Constitutions are much more than hierarchies of abstract norms. They have to do with how power is constituted, i.e., set up. Or, in the famous words of Harold Lasswell: "Who gets what, when, and how?"[11] As for constitutionalism, it refers to the mechanics of limiting the power of dominant social-political elites.[12] There is a verb-like quality to these concepts; both evoke relationships between living and breathing individuals rather than essences.

As for democracy, although most certainly a powerful aspirational ideal, it cannot be disassociated from the more prosaic reality of human struggles and conflicts. Professor Stephen Holmes states, for instance, that "... the most 'democratic' reason why elites have proved willing to impose limits on themselves is that such limits help to mobilize the voluntary cooperation of non-elites in the pursuit of the elite's most highly prized objectives, especially revenue extraction, victory in war, [and their holding on to power]."[13] This realistic approach to constitutionalism and democracy goes a long way in explaining the varying successes French-speaking Canadians in Quebec, French-speaking Canadians outside of Quebec, and Indigenous peoples respectively met with in their struggles, over time, to acquire a constitutionally guaranteed measure of autonomy.[14]

Federalism has also been plagued by definitions confining it to the regulation of orders of governments or of "peoples" and "nations."[15] Such definitions have the unfortunate effect of limiting the scope of the federal ideal. First, the peoples and nations mobilized in political and constitutional discourses are too often described as "subjective wholes" or abstract collective entities endowed with their own subjectivity and agency. Such definitions presume a political unanimity and cultural homogeneity between the members of said peoples and nations that is empirically contradicted every day. In this perspective, federalism becomes a clash between groups or governments irredeemably opposed to one another.

However, if we admit that single individuals sometimes cultivate multiple attachments and that the hierarchical organization of their identitary markers may vary according to circumstances, we are compelled to recognize that such individuals may consider themselves members of several distinct political communities without necessarily wanting to decide between them. Seen in this light, federalism can be conceived not simply as an *acknowledgment* of the existence of groups to which people attach themselves in various ways, but as a means to *structure* these group relationships and those of their members in order to allow for peaceful coexistence instead of continuous antagonism. Contrary to the concepts of nation, sovereignty, authenticity, and rights, federalism emphasizes the nature of the *relations* between persons and groups, rather than their *essence*.[16]

Our constitutional vocabulary therefore has a tendency to becloud the relational and human dimensions of our most fundamental constitutional concepts. In so doing, it makes it more difficult for members of the general public to understand their roles, and their responsibilities, in the production of law and constitutional law. Our future will require that law not be the exclusive preserve of state actors and institutions.

More tragically, conceptual reifications can exclude or "invisibilize" some important *de facto* constitutional actors. Apart from the Royal Proclamation of 1763 and the many treaties signed by the British and Canadian Crowns with Canada's Indigenous peoples, our constitutional texts have never, prior to 1982, recognized the latter peoples as constituent actors. On the contrary, when mentioned, as in paragraph 91(24) of the 1867 Constitution Act, they were confined to the status of legal objects rather than legal subjects. As for the non-human natural world, it is still but an object of law whose interests need not be taken into consideration, except as provincial and federal legislation allow for.

Finally, the four-year electoral cycle and the weekly or daily time-frame of everyday politics, combined to the inevitably massive equity implications of climate change (i.e., the complex distribution of the costs and benefits of adaptation and mitigation policies), kill all incentives for politicians to sponsor climate change policies whose material benefits will only be felt over the long run.[17] Future generations and the nonhuman natural world are not potential voters, still less constituent actors. We therefore know what is at stake, but the temptation to elude the truth is too strong.

Making the Invisible Visible

Part of the answer to the question whether Canadian federalism is fit to meet the challenges of the future rests on our ability to change our constitutional and legal discourses so as to make the invisible visible.

What will eventually compel us do so? Looking at the history of Western constitutionalism, Stephen Holmes defined as follows the one dominant political determinant in the advent of limited government: "If you wish a constitutional norm to govern the way politicians behave, you need to organize politically to give ruling groups an incentive to pay attention and accept the restraints on their own discretion for their benefit and yours."[18] Future generations may be voiceless, and the nonhuman natural world cannot organize politically; however, the latter can certainly get one's attention. Just watch the rising sea levels and listen to the screaming hurricane winds blowing down south.

What could be done then? In this short paper, I will confine myself to what could be addressed at a constitutional level.

I do not believe that judges have the legitimacy to bring about radical changes, but they could introduce a greater diversity in the aspirational ideals or common myths said to constitute the "fundamental and organizing principles" of the Canadian federation. By explicitly referring to the nonhuman natural world and to future generations, courts would draw these constituent actors out of their present constitutional invisibility and legitimize their future invocation in political-constitutional discourses.

In the *Secession Reference*, the Supreme Court identified democracy, federalism, constitutionalism and the rule of law, and respect for minorities as such foundational principles.[19] In the words of Yuval Noah Harari, author of *Sapiens: A Brief History of Humankind*, "[l]arge numbers of strangers can cooperate successfully by believing in common myths."[20] This is precisely the purpose of notions such as Canada's unwritten constitutional principles. As Harari notes, "lawyers are, in fact, powerful sorcerers. The principal difference between them and tribal shamans is that modern lawyers tell far stranger things."[21] He then goes on to examine the modern world's greatest legal myth, the corporation.

What would happen if the protection of the nonhuman natural world and and of future generations were added to the list of our foundational principles, of our common myths?[22] First of all, it could open up a space within Canada's legal-constitutional thinking for Indigenous legal-constitutional traditions that *do*, in their very vocabulary and substance, apprehend land as a source of law.[23] Anishinaabe law, for instance, is partly developed from observation of the physical world.[24] If such Indigenous legal traditions were allowed to permeate our general understanding of law, it could lead us to endow natural physical entities with specific legal interests.

This might sound farfetched for some, but in the recent *Whanganui River Claims Settlement Act* enacted in 2017,[25] the government of New Zealand, after long negotiations with the Maoris, recognized the *Te Awa Tupua* – the Whanganui River, the country's longest navigable river – as a hybrid juristic person,[26] i.e., as both a living entity[27] and a corporate one.[28] Long before that, the Judicial Committee of the Privy Council itself had already recognized that a "disinterested next friend" could be appointed by a court of law to represent the interests of an Hindu idol, claiming that the latter was a "juristic entity" that, according to the religious customs of the Hindus, had a "juridical status with the power of suing and being sued."[29]

Second, it might be worthwhile for courts to engage with the fact that, while Indigenous peoples were indeed the first humans to occupy this land, Indigenous legal traditions themselves give temporal priority of occupation to nonhuman natural entities.[30] If the purpose of section 35 of the 1982 Constitution Act[31] is to foster the development of a truly "intersocietal law," as claimed by the Supreme Court of Canada,[32] then Indigenous legal traditions could provide the legal basis for the recognition of some rights to the nonhuman natural world.

Third, the Supreme Court has already invoked an Indigenous foundational principle, i.e., that human activity over a territory burdened by an aboriginal title should not be "irreconcilable with the ability of succeeding generations to benefit from the land."[33] However, the Court used this principle in a very cynical way. This "inherent limit" of irreconcilability, as I just mentioned, was said to apply only to the use made by Indigenous communities holding titles to the land, or to uses of lands so burdened by private operators holding permits from either the Provincial or Federal Crowns.[34] In other words, the need for developers to take into consideration the interests of future generations only applies to development of aboriginal title land, and not to development elsewhere. Nine judges and thirty-six law clerks did not realize how unbelievably odd it was not to hold all operators to the same requirements even where no aboriginal titles were involved!

Furthermore, according to the Court's reasoning, the burden of protecting the earth for future generations falls upon the shoulders of Canada's Indigenous peoples, or more particularly, those Indigenous communities who can find the tens of millions of dollars needed for litigation necessary to establish an aboriginal title – since, as we just said, the "seventh generation principle" only applies to lands so burdened. Indigenous peoples have borne the brunt of the distributive inequities of economic development (shouldering the costs without gaining much of the benefits), they should not now bear the burden of saving us from the abyss.

Still, courts could resort to the "seventh generation principle" in a manner honouring both the Indigenous peoples, the non-natural human world and future generations (and all living Canadians for that matter!). For instance, in the recent *Ktunaxa* case,[35] British Columbia approved the construction of a ski resort on a territory of spiritual significance for the Ktunaxa who believed it to be inhabited by the Grizzly Bear Spirit, a being central to Ktunaxa religious beliefs and cosmology. The Court concluded that the ski resort's construction did not breach the Ktunaxa's freedom of religion and that sufficient consultation and accommodation had been achieved to meet the requirements established under Section 35 of the Constitution Act, 1982.

Strangely enough, although the justices speaking for the majority admitted that "the goal of the process [of consultation was] reconciliation of the Aboriginal and state interest,"[36] never once did they mention what particular public interest was served by British Columbia's Land Act and Ministry of Lands, Parks and Housing Act. The concurring justices were a little more precise, mentioning that the Minister of Forests' statutory objectives consisted in administering Crown lands and disposing of them in the public interest.[37]

But still, why should the public interest be immediately conflated with economic development? Why should any form of economic development – even ones designed to please the rich among the rich – be immediately presumed "reconcilable with the ability of succeeding generations to benefit from the land"? Why should the Court implicitly enshrine, as it does, economic and property rights in our Constitution? Why couldn't the Court entertain the idea that "Indigenous rights and interests need not be seen as adverse to the interests of all other Canadians – indeed they may encompass them"?[38]

Conclusion

I am not naïve. I entertain a very realist understanding of law in general and of constitutional law in particular. I do not know if judges and legislators will eventually embrace a long-term perspective. But in thinking about the "exceptional" times we will shortly be facing, I am reminded of Carl Schmitt's aphorism according to which "[s]overeign is he who decides on the exception."[39] He goes on to explain: "Therein resides the essence of the state's sovereignty, which must be juristically defined correctly, not as the monopoly to coerce or to rule, but as the monopoly to decide. The exception reveals most clearly the essence of the state's authority."[40] My belief is that in the exceptional contest between humankind and Nature we are about to face, the former does not stand a good chance of deciding on the exception. We will eventually know who the true sovereign is, and we might not like its ultimate decisions.

NOTES

1 The following is adapted from a paper delivered at the *Canada and its Centennial and Sesquicentennial Conference,* University of Toronto, November 17–18, 2017. The author thanks Michel Morin, Sophie Thériault, Hugo Tremblay, Elizabeth Steyn, Sofia Panaccio, and most especially John Borrows for their helpful comments.
2 John Borrows, *Canada's Indigenous Constitution* (Toronto: University of Toronto Press, 2010), 158.

3   Boris Cyrulnik, "Je suis optimiste puisqu'on court à la catastrophe," *Regain 2012*, http://www.regain2012.com/2016/04/je-suis-optimiste-puisqu-on-court-a-la-catastrophe-1.html.

4   Winston S. Churchill, *Memoirs of the Second World War. An abridgement of the six volumes of the Second World War* (Boston: Houghton Mifflin Company, 1959), 12.

5   Michelle Bilodeau, "How David Suzuki Thinks Humans Can Sustainably Co-exist with the Earth at This Point," *CBC Life*, October 11, 2017, http://www.cbc.ca/life/wellness/how-david-suzuki-thinks-humans-can-sustainably-coexist-with-the-earth-at-this-point-1.4349450. See also William J. Ripple, Christopher Wolf, Thomas M. Newsome, Mauro Galetti, Mohammed Alamgir, Eileen Crist, Mahmoud I. Mahmoud, William F. Laurance, and 15,364 scientist signatories from 184 countries, "World Scientists' Warning to Humanity: A Second Notice," *BioScience* 67, no. 12 (December 2017): 1026–8.

6   On the impact of changing a noun into a verb, see John Borrows, "Anishinaabe Language and Law," unpublished manuscript.

7   Lon L. Fuller, "Freedom: A Suggested Analysis," *Harvard Law Review* 68, no. 8 (1955): 1305–25 at 1322.

8   Jean Leclair, "Military Historiography, Warriors and Soldiers: The Normative Impact of Epistemological Choices," in *From Recognition to Reconciliation: Essays on the Constitutional Entrenchment of Aboriginal and Treaty Rights*, ed. Patrick Macklem and Douglas Sanderson (Toronto: University of Toronto Press, 2016), 179.

9   Jennifer Nedelsky, "Reconceiving Rights as Relationship," *Review of Constitutional Studies* 1 (1994 1993): 8.

10 Martin Loughlin, *The Idea of Public Law* (Oxford: Oxford University Press, 2003), 81.

11 Harold Lasswell, *Politics: Who Gets What, When, and How* (Cleveland: Meridian, 1958).

12 Stephen Holmes, "Constitutions and Constitutionalism," in *The Oxford Handbook of Comparative Constitutional Law*, ed. Mark Rosenfeld and Andras *Sajó* (Oxford: Oxford University Press, 2012), 189.

13 Stephen Holmes, "Constitutions and Constitutionalism," 199.

14 Jean Leclair, "The Story of Constitutions, Constitutionalism and Reconciliation: A Work of Prose? Poetry? Or Both?," *Review of Constitutional Studies* 22, no. 3 (2017): 329–46.

15 Jean Leclair, "*Ceintures fléchées* and Wampum Belts: Quebec and Indigenous Peoples in the Canadian Federation," *Journal of Parliamentary and Political Law*, Special Issue Canada's Constitutional and Governace Challenges after 150 Years (2018): 17–21.

16 Jean Leclair, "Envisaging Canada in a Disenchanted World: Reflections on Federalism, Nationalism, and Distinctive Indigenous Identity," *Constitutional Forum* 25 (2016): 15–28.

17 For an overview of what confronting climate change entails, see James Meadowcroft, "Climate Change Governance," *World Bank Policy Research Working Paper*, no. 4941 (May 1, 2009), https://papers.ssrn.com/abstract=1407959.N. For a Canada-focused analysis, see Natural Resources Canada, "Re-Energizing Canada: Pathways to a Low-Carbon Future," Dialogues on Sustainability, 2016, http://www.sustainablecanadadialogues.ca/en/scd/energy.

18 Stephen Holmes, "Constitutions and Constitutionalism," 215.

19 *Reference re Secession of Quebec*, [1998] 2 S.C.R. 217, 1998 SCC 793 (CanLII).

20 Yuval Noah Harari, *Sapiens: A Brief History of Humankind* (Toronto: McClelland & Stewart, 2014), 27.

21 Harari, *Sapiens*, 28.

22 As to what could be envisaged from a non-Indigenous point of view, see Hugo Tremblay, "Pour une équité intergénérationnelle" in *Sauvons la justice! 39 propositions pour agir*, ed. Catherine Régis, Karim Benyekhlef, Daniel Weinstock (Montréal: Del Busso Éditeur, 2017), 194.

23 John Borrows, "Anishinaabe Language and Law," unpublished manuscript; John Borrows, "Indigenous Constitutionalism: Pre-Existing legal Genealogies in Canada," in *The Oxford Handbook of the Canadian Constitution*, ed. Peter Oliver, Patrick Macklem, Nathalie Des Rosiers (Oxford: Oxford University Press, 2017), 13.

24 Borrows, "Anishinaabe Language."

25 *Te Awa Tupua (Whanganui River Claims Settlement) Act*, No. 7 of 2017, s 3(b) and (c).

26 *Te Awa Tupua (Whanganui River Claims Settlement) Act*, Part 2.

27 *Te Awa Tupua (Whanganui River Claims Settlement) Act*, s 12.

28 *Te Awa Tupua (Whanganui River Claims Settlement) Act*, s 17 (a)–(g).

29 *Pramatha Nath Mullick v. Pradvumna Kumar Mullick*, (1925) L.R. 52; Ind. App. 245, at par. 8: "A Hindu idol is, according to long established authority, founded upon the religious customs of the Hindus, and the recognition thereof by Courts of law, a 'juristic entity.' It has a juridical status with the power of suing and being sued. Its interests are attended to by the person who has the deity in his charge and who is in law its manager with all the powers which would, in such circumstances, on analogy, be given to the manager of the estate of an infant heir, (sic) It is unnecessary to quote the authorities; for this doctrine, thus simply stated, is firmly established."

30 John Borrows, "Indigenous Law and Governance: Challenging Pre-Contact and Post-Contact Distinctions in Canadian Constitutional Law?" in *Les Conférences Chevrette-Marx/The Chevrette-Marx Lectures* (Montréal: Thémis, 2017), 17–18.

31 This section states that "[t]he existing aboriginal and treaty rights of the aboriginal peoples of Canada are hereby recognized and affirmed" and sub-section 35(2) specifies that "'aboriginal peoples of Canada' includ[e] the Indian, Inuit and Métis peoples of Canada."

32 *R. v. Van der Peet*, [1996] 2 S.C.R. 507, 1996 SCC 216 (CanLII), para. 42.

33 *Tsilhqot'in Nation v. British Columbia*, [2014] 2 S.C.R. 257, 2014 SCC 44 (CanLII), para. 74.

34 *Tsilhqot'in Nation v. British Columbia*, [2014] 2 S.C.R. 257, 2014 SCC 44 (CanLII), paras. 74 and 86.

35 *Ktunaxa Nation v. British Columbia (Forests, Lands and Natural Resource Operations)*, 2017 SCC 54 (CanLII).

36 *Ktunaxa Nation v. British Columbia (Forests, Lands and Natural Resource Operations)*, para. 114.

37 *Ktunaxa Nation v. British Columbia (Forests, Lands and Natural Resource Operations)*, para. 152.

38 Natasha Bakht and Lynda Collins, "'The Earth Is Our Mother': Freedom of Religion and the Preservation of Indigenous Sacred Sites in Canada," *McGill Law Journal* 62, no. 3 (2017): 777–812. Interestingly, "New Democrat MP Wayne Stetski, whose constituency includes the Ktunaxa, told the [Toronto] Star in an interview 'the majority of my constituents do not support' the project and neither does he. 'I don't think we need another downhill ski area in my riding – we have ten already if I remember the count – so from my perspective, this area is really important to the Ktunaxa; I'd like to see it stay in its natural state.'" Tonda MacCharles, "Supreme Court Approves B.C. Ski Resort Development on Indigenous Lands," *Toronto Star*, November 2, 2017, https://www.thestar.com/news/canada/2017/11/02/supreme-court-approves-bc-ski-resort-development-on-indigenous-lands.html.

39 Carl Schmitt, *Political Theology: Four Chapters on the Concept of Sovereignty*, trans. George Schwab (Chicago: University of Chicago Press, 2005), 8.

40 Schmitt, 13.

13 Canadian Federalism, Canadian Allegiance, and Economic Inequality

JEREMY WEBBER

I start with two great truths about federal systems of government.

First, their primary purpose is to organize the exercise of democratic self-determination. Their role is not simply to allow for policy differentiation at different levels of the state. That is epiphenomenal, not primary. Their primary role is to organize democratic agency so that citizens can govern themselves through engagement in two overlapping political communities.[1]

The test of a healthy federal system is therefore the health of each of these levels as arenas for democratic self-government. That means that one must attend to questions of democratic legitimacy, political participation, and the practical conditions of effective citizenship at both levels of government. The preconditions of democratic sovereignty and allegiance are crucial elements in our assessment of the continuing viability of federal structures of government.

We saw the role of such an emphasis on democratic participation in the great constitutional debates of the centennial era. That was a time of significant democratization of Canadian political life, especially in Quebec where, through the Quiet Revolution, francophone Quebecers sought to use the state as never before to serve as their agent in the pursuit of collectively-determined ends, and in Ottawa, where successive governments sought to make the federal level a forum for the political engagement of francophone as well as anglophone Canadians. The era saw, then, the simultaneous redefinition of both levels of government as forums for democratic self-government, seeking to make them genuinely accessible to their francophone as well as their anglophone citizens. This transformation of French Canadian participation in political life drove the debates over Canadian federalism in the 1960s and 1970s.

But even beyond the concerns of Quebec, the 1960s and 1970s were a period of democratization in Canadian life – a time of citizens' participation in great social projects, and during which the principal elements of Canadian social programs and educational institutions were laid down and extended.

Now, Charles Taylor famously distinguished the participation of Quebecers in the federal polity from that of other Canadians by suggesting that francophone Quebecers participated in Canada *through* the collectivity of Quebec – as though their engagement and allegiance to Canada were indirect.[2] I don't disagree with Charles Taylor over much, but this characterization, I think, is wrong. It is belied by the fact that francophone Quebecers participated actively and prominently in political developments at the federal as well as the provincial level. Indeed, they often simultaneously pursued different political strategies at both levels, a difference epitomized by their election of Liberal governments in Ottawa and Parti Québécois governments in Quebec. The period of Canada's centennial saw, in other words, the reconfiguration of democratic political life at both levels in a manner that consolidated allegiance to both.

The second great truth of federal political systems is that it is a mistake to focus only on the formal definition of legislative powers. One also has to follow the money.

The central issues of federal-provincial relations often revolve around taxation and expenditure – both the entitlement of each level to raise revenue and decide its expenditure (the preconditions of the effective exercise of government powers) and, in the democratic practice of federalism, the practical flow of burdens and benefits between citizens and their governments. That was manifestly the case in debates over the division of powers in the 1960s and beyond. There was conscious competition – and often collaboration – between levels of government in the development of Canada's foundational social programs. And the frictions that arose over the division of powers focused overwhelmingly on Ottawa's use of the spending power: its ability to pursue very significant programs within areas of provincial jurisdiction, due to the extensive fiscal resources it controls relative to its constitutional responsibilities.

During the centennial era and the constitutional debates that followed, the specific manifestation of those two great truths was largely settled, though not without cost. That was true even in Quebec, where the province was permanently transformed by the Quiet Revolution and Ottawa was made a genuine government for francophone as well as anglophone Canadians. The manner in which the Canadian constitution was patriated – and, above all, the subsequent rejection of the Meech Lake Accord by many anglophone Canadians – dampened the enthusiasm with which francophone Quebecers embraced a restructured Canada. I suspect that some of the psychological disengagement of Quebecers – the "decanadianization" of Quebecers that Parti Québécois leader Jean-François Lisée has described and, of course, advocated – may be permanent, only partially alleviated by the fact that all but one of the Meech Lake Accord's elements have been subsequently accepted as working assumptions of the Canadian political order.[3] But, with that important qualification, the ground rules of contemporary Canadian federalism have largely been settled. There is no great appetite, even in Quebec, for renewed constitutional negotiations.

So what, then, about the future of Canadian federalism? I think we stand on the edge of a new set of challenges – an equally serious set of challenges – grounded in the same two truths of federal governance.

An important dimension of healthy, self-governing, democratic polities is a kind of social contract: the perception that citizens bear a roughly equivalent balance of the benefits and burdens of citizenship. It was no accident that the vibrant transformation of the federal system in the 1960s and 1970s, for example, coincided with a period of rising wages, the development of our foundational social programs, and a greater equality of after-tax income among Canadians than pertains today. The health of democratic institutions depends on a rough and ready equality among citizens. That equality may not be – indeed never is – complete equality of outcomes, but nor is it reducible to the formal equality of the right to vote. There is a fiscal dimension to citizens' equality – a sense that the burdens and benefits of citizenship are being fairly shared. If burdens and benefits appear to citizens to be wildly skewed, trust in political institutions is eroded, and their ability to claim the allegiance of their citizens undermined.

With the relative weakening of successive federal governments' commitment to policies that promote income equality, are we beginning to see the erosion of political engagement and political allegiance, with potentially devastating consequences for our federally organized democratic communities?

We see what that erosion can lead to in the phenomenon south of the border. Donald Trump's victory in the presidential race resulted in part from the enduring racism of segments of American society, with that racism reacting against the Obama presidency – a presidency that had produced an increase in political engagement by African-Americans and Latinos. And there was also more than a little misogyny in the backlash against the candidacy of Hillary Clinton. But those things weren't all that was going on. The underperformance of the Clinton campaign in key Democratic constituencies was in significant measure a product of the venality of so much of contemporary politics – the sense that American politics is skewed towards those with wealth, a perception to which Hillary Clinton appeared to be especially tone-deaf. It is difficult to pose as the champion of beleaguered citizens when you charge ten times their annual income to deliver a speech. While it was perverse of citizens to think that Trump might do better, the evidence of disaffection with the political system was clear.[4]

In Canada we have thus far escaped such a significant erosion of political trust, and the signs that do exist of political erosion are materially different from those in the United States. But nevertheless, there are signs in Canada of growing alienation from conventional politics among those who observe that the burdens and benefits of economic citizenship are skewed. We saw it in the traction that the Occupy Movement attained in Canada. We have witnessed the rise of political parties, such as the Green Party, that consciously define themselves as championing interests that are neglected by the established parties. Above all, we struggle to persuade young people that voting is worth their while.

I don't suggest that the battle for the legitimacy of our institutions is lost. In that regard, the developments in Indigenous politics are instructive. Idle No More embodied many of the elements of a politics of the disaffected. But interestingly that energy was also directed into an attempt to transform Indigenous engagement in Canadian politics so that today, in both Canada and my province, the political agenda is strongly shaped by Indigenous ministers: first, at the federal level, by the Minister of Justice, Jody Wilson-Raybould; and second in British Columbia, by the Minister of Finance and Deputy Premier, Carole James, and the Minister of Advanced Education, Melanie Mark.

That experience should remind us that it is a mistake to assume that direct action is antithetical to electoral politics. It often serves to mobilize citizens for political engagement of all kinds, as indeed Occupy did for many of its activists. However, we should not be complacent about the signs of disaffection. Part of what is happening may be that outsiders are putting engagement in the Canadian political order to the test. If it fails, we may see a lasting disengagement.

So, what does this have to do with our federal structures?

If we care about self-government at all, the hollowing out of citizens' engagement must be cause for concern. But there is also a more specific effect on the central preoccupations of federalism. In Canada, as with so much else, political alienation has a federal-provincial dimension.

First, many of the tools that have, or that could have, historically promoted greater equality in Canada have been the responsibility of the federal government. I am not thinking principally of the federal creation of social programs, although that certainly is part of the story. I accept that the aggressive use of the federal spending power created significant strains in Canadian federalism and I support the limitations that the Meech Lake Accord would have placed on its use.[5] Rather, I have in mind the most important equality-promoting tool that Ottawa possesses, namely its effective control over the income taxation system. Ottawa also deploys equalization payments, its jurisdictions with respect to the north and Indigenous peoples, and its control over macroeconomic policy. Its pursuit of greater equality-producing programs in these areas has at times been fundamental to the consolidation of allegiance to the federal level of government. If it is perceived to be abandoning that role, we may see – we may well be seeing – a reciprocal disengagement by increasing numbers of citizens. The equality consequences of the choice of policy instrument discussed by John Myles and Daniel Béland in this volume have important impacts on allegiance and engagement.

Moreover, the federal government is also the privileged custodian of the most visible emblems of fairness in the distribution of burdens and benefits among citizens. One of the most significant corrosive issues of our age is the evasion of the social contract by those with the wealth and the will to play the inter-jurisdictional taxation game, an avoidance of responsibility that occurs with the apparent connivance of our federal governments, who ensure that much of that activity (but not all of it) is legal. That phenomenon dramatizes, in ways that the gradual increase of inequality in Canadian society cannot do, the perception that those with wealth who would rather not shoulder the burdens of citizenship will get an easy ride by their friends in government. It has a distinct Canadian dimension, exposed in previous revelations about the use of offshore trusts and recently reinforced by the Paradise Papers. One gets the impression that the federal government's stock strategy is to speak platitudes, plead its supposed inability to act without international coordination, and treat the issue as at most a quarrel among Canadian political parties. But I suspect that, more than any other issue, it has the capacity to undermine Canadians' sense of the basic fairness of their political institutions.

For many Canadians who do not have a strong parallel pole of allegiance, such disaffection may only result, in the short run, in disengagement from the political process. That general disengagement should of course be a matter of deep concern to us, but in Quebec, where there is a rival claimant to nationhood, might it also contribute to a shift in the balance of Quebecers' allegiance?

If that seems farfetched, think of the impact that the perception of corruption has historically had on support for secession in Quebec: the great progress, for example, that the Parti Québécois made because of its long demonstration of governmental rectitude, or the collapse of federal Liberal support in Quebec as a result of the sponsorship scandal. If one looks internationally, some of the best analyses of the rise of the Catalonian independence movement also emphasize the coincidence of economic downturn with the collapse of the legitimacy of Spanish institutions as a result of a series of corruption scandals.[6] We now see significantly more attention being paid to issues of economic fairness by the Quebec government, where a perception of social solidarity, grounded in social policy, has long had significant purchase. We see Quebec's greater concern with fiscal fairness in its greater willingness to address multinationals' avoidance of sales tax. Are these signs of a pulling apart of attention to fiscal fairness in Canada and Quebec?

Robert Bourassa, when he was Quebec's Premier, used the phrase "fédéralisme rentable" to emphasize that Quebecers should remain in Canada based on the fiscal benefits flowing to Quebec. Bourassa's phrase captured the importance of the fiscal dimensions of federalism, but it conceived of those relations entirely as an economic calculation of cost and benefit. That, I think, misses the principal point, for Quebecers as for other Canadians.[7] Fiscal relations are important because they are the outward manifestation of a deeper social contract.

Of course, the significance of these issues goes well beyond their impact on the relationship of Quebec to the rest of Canada. The fair distribution of benefits and burdens of citizenship is important for its own sake. Nevertheless, when I try to identify likely long-term challenges to the health of our federal system, they are tied to questions of allegiance and engagement. Those in turn are currently being reshaped by our governments' weak commitment to economic equality.

NOTES

1 See Richard Simeon's classic article: Richard E. Simeon, "Criteria for Choice in Federal Systems," *Queen's Law Journal* 8 (1981 1982): 131–57.

2 Charles Taylor, *Reconciling the Solitudes: Essays on Canadian Federalism and Nationalism*, ed. Guy Laforest (Montreal: McGill-Queen's University Press, 1993), 182–3.

3 On decanadianization, see Rhéal Séguin, "PQ Touts Quebec's 'Decanadianization,' Citing New Poll's Findings," *The Globe and Mail*, December 11, 2013, https://www.theglobeandmail.com/news/politics/pq-touts-quebecs-decanadianization-citing-new-polls-findings/article15905393/. On the constitutional discussions of the 1980s and 1990s, see Jeremy Webber, *Reimagining Canada: Language, Culture, Community, and the Canadian Constitution* (Montreal: McGill-Queen's University Press, 1994). For Meech Lake's belated success, see Jeremy Webber, "The Delayed (and Qualified) Victory of the Meech Lake Accord: The Role of Constitutional Reform in Undermining and Restoring Intercommunal Trust," in *Trust, Distrust, and Mistrust in Multinational Democracies: Comparative Perspectives*, ed. Dimitrios Karmis and François Rocher (Montreal: McGill-Queen's University Press, 2018), 166–209.

4 The phenomenon is not limited to the United States. See the collapse of the Social Mobility Commission in the United Kingdom in Michael Savage, "Theresa May Faces New Crisis after Mass Walkout over Social Policy," *The Guardian*, December 3, 2017, http://www.theguardian.com/politics/2017/dec/02/theresa-may-crisis-mass-walkout-social-policy-alan-milburn.

5 See note 3 supra.

6 Francisco Colom, "The Spanish Transition Forty Years Later: Democracy, Devolution and Pluralism," Global Centre for Pluralism, May 2017, https://www.pluralism.ca/press-release/spanish-transition-forty-years-later-democracy-devolution-pluralism/.

7 See the poll reported at the height of the post-Meech crisis in the issue of *L'actualité* entitled "Le Canada dans le peau," *L'actualité* 17, no. 11 (July 1992), 21–52.

14 Indigenous-Canadian Relations at the Sesquicentennial: An Opportunity for Real and Lasting Transformation

SHERYL LIGHTFOOT

At Canada's centennial anniversary in 1967, it had only been seven years since status Indians were granted the right to vote in Canada without losing their Indian status. And it had only been sixteen years since the most restrictive aspects of the Indian Act had been lifted, including prohibitions on dances, ceremonies, and the ban on the pursuit of land claims.[1] While Canada was celebrating its 100th birthday, Indigenous peoples took the opportunity to highlight the injustices they had suffered over those 100 years.

On July 1, 1967, Tsleil-Waututh Chief Dan George addressed a crowd of 32,000 people gathered at Empire Stadium in Vancouver to celebrate Canada's centennial. The speech he gave, "Lament for Confederation," not only stunned the crowd into reflective silence, it subsequently served as an important and lasting reminder of the experience of Indigenous peoples in twentieth-century Canada:

> How long have I known you, Oh Canada? A hundred years? Yes, a hundred years. And many, many seelanum more. And today, when you celebrate your hundred years, Oh Canada, I am sad for all the Indian people throughout the land ... But in the long hundred years since the white man came, I have seen my freedom disappear like the salmon going mysteriously out to sea. The white man's strange customs, which I could not understand, pressed down upon me until I could no longer breathe.[2]

Now, as we recognize Canada's sesquicentennial fifty years later, we pause to consider the multiple challenges faced by the relationship between Indigenous peoples and Canada. We can examine the opportunity to move in a positive direction in terms of that relationship, or rather, relationships, between Indigenous peoples and this country we call Canada. At the centre of this opportunity is the *United Nations Declaration on the Rights of Indigenous Peoples*, a document that, if implemented in Canada, can reshape this relationship for the better.

Some massive changes occurred in the Indigenous-Canadian relationship between 1967 and today. The Liberal government of Pierre Trudeau ushered in many social changes in its quest for the "just society," including major changes to Indian Affairs. By Pierre Trudeau's calculations, the policies that segregated Indians in Canada had clearly failed – and therefore, he reasoned, the just society for Indigenous peoples would be achieved through complete desegregation, the scrapping of Indian status, and the elimination of any special Indian policies and programs. As Trudeau noted at the time:

> We can go on adding bricks of discrimination around the ghetto in which they live and, at the same time, perhaps helping them preserve certain cultural traits and certain ancestral rights. Or, we can say, you're at a crossroad – the time is now to decide whether the Indians will be a race apart in Canada or whether they will be Canadians of full status.[3]

The result of this reasoning was the now notorious White Paper, drafted by Indian Affairs Minister Jean Chrétien and presented to Parliament in 1969.[4] The White Paper was a top-down initiative of a government that purported to provide a solution to Indigenous peoples' problems and was, as a result, not exactly embraced by Indigenous people. Instead, it unleashed a wave of Indigenous protest and activism through the 1970s and early 80s the likes of which this country had never witnessed. This wave of activism resulted in an important positive shift: Section 35 of the Constitution Act, 1982, while far from perfect in how it has been interpreted by the courts, did provide some measure of protection for Aboriginal and treaty rights.

Then came 1990, and Oka. In March of that year, the Mohawks of Kanesatake set up a blockade to prevent bulldozers from breaking ground for a golf course expansion planned on a Mohawk burial ground. On July 11, 1990, the mayor of Oka called in the provincial police to enforce a Quebec superior court injunction to have the blockade removed. The next day, 100 heavily-armed police officers arrived at the blockade. Tensions ran extremely high and gunfire eventually erupted, killing a police officer. Tensions increased through the summer, and a blockade was set up on the Mercier Bridge into Montreal by sympathizers with the Mohawks of Kanesatake's cause. The Canadian

Army was called in by mid-August to face down the Mohawk warriors. On August 29, the Mercier Bridge blockade was removed, and by the end of September, a deal was struck whereby the barricades came down in return for cancellation of the golf course expansion.[5]

During and after the Oka crisis, it became obvious that even Section 35 of the 1982 Constitution was inadequate to address the scope of Indigenous issues in Canada, particularly the rights of Indigenous peoples to land and self-determination. While Canada tried to absorb the reality of its army being deployed against a land rights occupation at Kanasatake, the Royal Commission on Aboriginal Peoples reshaped the Indigenous-Canadian relationship yet again. The final 4,000-page report of the Royal Commission, issued in 1996 in five volumes, recommended numerous alterations in the Canada-Indigenous relationship, including the expansion of Indigenous land base and land rights, enhancement of structures of governance for Indigenous peoples, new legislation, and the creation of numerous initiatives to address the health, social, and educational needs of Indigenous peoples.[6]

The Idle No More movement of 2012–13 showed us, yet again, how far we have to go. What began as teach-ins and protests around Saskatchewan against a series of proposed parliamentary bills that would erode both environmental protections and Indigenous sovereignty quickly became "one of the largest Indigenous mass movements in Canadian history – sparking hundreds of teach-ins, rallies, and protests" across Canada and the world.[7]

Today, Canada stands at yet another a crossroads in its relationship with Indigenous peoples. An incredible opportunity lies before us for a better future. A guiding framework exists – a framework that Indigenous peoples and states designed, drafted, and negotiated together over three full decades: the *United Nations Declaration on the Rights of Indigenous Peoples*.[8] While it is not a perfect document, it provides a roadmap for a substantially improved relationship.

Canada now has the opportunity to reset and renew its relationship with Indigenous peoples and to ground that relationship in principles of cooperation, partnership, mutual respect, consent, justice, and human rights – to meet the nation-to-nation intent of the original treaty relations between the early arrivals from Europe and the powerful Indigenous nations they first encountered and made cooperative treaties with.

In my 2016 book, *Global Indigenous Rights and Politics: A Subtle Revolution*, I argue that Indigenous rights, if implemented, are transformational in a number of ways.[9] This set of transformations is potentially revolutionary, not only for Indigenous state relations, but also for international relations, in both theory and practice.

In terms of the Indigenous-Canadian relationship, the potential trans-formative shift lies in the guiding framework that the *UN Declaration on the Rights of Indigenous Peoples* provides.[10] An Indigenous-Canada rela-tionship that aligns with the expectations of the *UN Declaration* would provide more equality, greater justice, enhanced democracy, lower con-flict, and bring Canada into compliance with this global human rights standard. Canada could in turn potentially lead the world in doing so.

The *UN Declaration* is in many ways a remedial document, intended to rectify the widespread systematic denial of human rights to Indig-enous peoples in both national and global contexts. But it is also very forward looking, and provides a guiding framework for the proper di-rection of future relationships between states and Indigenous peoples around the world.

According to the *UN Declaration*, relationships between states and In-digenous peoples should be characterized by the following key principles:

- Full equality of Indigenous peoples, meaning non-discrimination in all facets of government and society;
- Rights to protect and restore Indigenous cultures, languages, spirit-uality, education, and institutions, including the state's obligation to assist with those efforts;
- Equal self-determination of Indigenous peoples as peoples;
- Recognition and respect for land rights, including restitution where possible and appropriate, and redress otherwise;
- Free, prior, and informed consent (FPIC) over all issues that impact Indigenous peoples; and
- A nation-to-nation political relationship.

So, where is Canada, at the moment, on this journey?

In June 2015, Canada's Truth and Reconciliation Commission (TRC) released its Summary Report, which included ninety-four "Calls to Ac-tion."[11] These recommendations call upon all levels of government to make fundamental changes in policies and programs in order to repair the harm caused by residential schools. Central to these recommenda-tions is a call for all levels of government to fully adopt and implement the *UN Declaration* as the framework for reconciliation in Canada, in-cluding within a national action plan. In total, twelve of the ninety-four Calls to Action referenced the *UN Declaration*.

The *UN Declaration* became an issue during the 2015 federal elec-tion, which was launched in mid-summer 2015 on the heels of the June TRC announcement. Justin Trudeau promised immediate action on the

TRC's ninety-four calls to action and promised that his government would start implementing the *UN Declaration*.[12]

The newly elected Prime Minister crafted a cabinet that included two Indigenous members, and his mandate letters to ministers included directives to implement the recommendations of the TRC including implementation of the *UN Declaration*, stating that "no relationship is more important to me and to Canada than the one with Indigenous peoples."[13]

In May 2016, both Justice Minister Jody Wilson-Raybould and Indian Affairs Minister Carolyn Bennett went to New York to address the United Nations Permanent Forum on Indigenous Issues. Wilson-Raybould spoke at the opening ceremony with a special statement on Canada's new position on the *UN Declaration*, the Indian Act, reconciliation, and FPIC. She said that Canada needed to reform the ways it conducts business with Indigenous peoples, stressing the central role the *UN Declaration* should play in that reordering and renewal.[14]

The next day, Indian Affairs Minister Carolyn Bennett addressed the UN Permanent Forum. She announced that Canada would hereafter be a "full supporter of the Declaration, without qualification." Following loud applause and a standing ovation, she continued: "we intend nothing less than to adopt and implement the Declaration."[15]

In the meantime, New Democratic Party Member of Parliament Romeo Saganash tabled Bill C-262, titled "UN Declaration on the Rights of Indigenous Peoples Act," a piece of legislation that if passed would ensure that the laws of Canada respect the *UN Declaration*.[16] This bill sets out the key principles that will guide implementation of the *UN Declaration* in Canada. It provides "clear public affirmation" that the standards of the *UN Declaration* will have "application in Canadian law." It requires a review of all federal legislation to ensure full consistency with the *UN Declaration*. It also requires that the federal government collaborate with Indigenous peoples to develop both a national action plan for implementation and annual implementation progress reports to Parliament. In November 2017, Justice Minister Jody Wilson-Raybould announced government support for Bill C-262.[17]

In February 2017, Prime Minister Trudeau established a ministerial working group to review all laws and policies related to Indigenous peoples, headed by Minister Wilson-Raybould.[18] After five months of work, the group (composed entirely of sitting government personnel and no representatives of Indigenous peoples or organizations) released ten principles respecting the government of Canada's relationship with Indigenous peoples which were said to articulate the broad contours of what implementation of the *UN Declaration* should look like in Canada.[19]

In the spring of 2017, Minister Bennett stated at the UN Permanent Forum on Indigenous Issues that Canada would now support the principle of FPIC without reservations, retracting all of the previous government's concerns.[20] If true, the result would be a tremendous leap forward in implementation. But the federal government has not provided any specifics or follow-up announcements about FPIC. Crucially, government has made no changes to laws, policies, or practices that might indicate a change in policy stance.

In August 2017, the Prime Minister announced that the Indigenous Affairs ministry would be split in two: one ministry for service delivery, to be headed by former Health Minister Jane Philpott, and another for Crown-Indigenous relations, to be led by Minister Bennett.[21] Indigenous voices from across country, and especially on social media, said: "Why? We never asked for this? Why didn't anyone ask us if implementation should include two Indigenous ministries?" "So now we have two bosses and still no implementation?" "Where is the consultation?"

The Trudeau government has made many lofty promises and proclaimed the best of intentions using all the right language. But after nearly two years in power, it faces increasing criticism from Indigenous circles about the lack of substantive change that has been thinly veiled under beautiful rhetoric. The government's lack of consultation with Indigenous peoples over the process of change has been noted.

Canada is truly standing at a crossroads with respect to Indigenous rights. On the one hand, Canada's ruling party and Prime Minister have stated a clear intention to respond to the 94 Calls to Action of the Truth and Reconciliation Commission. It has promised to chart a new course with Indigenous peoples based on the *UN Declaration on the Rights of Indigenous Peoples*. On the other hand, Canada is hesitant. This visionary government has yet to develop any viable national implementation plan.

Under the *UN Declaration*, the history of settler state dispossession of Indigenous peoples can no longer be considered legitimate, nor can colonial administration, or "rule over" Indigenous peoples, by such statutes as the Indian Act. Indigenous self-determination, including consent, must be respected on an equal basis with the rights of all other peoples in Canada. The *UN Declaration* has called for nothing short of full-scale and fundamental change of all existing systems – laws, policies, programs, and full systems of governance. While the rhetoric is right, it seems that real steps toward substantive change may still be a long way off.

This government has the opportunity to keep moving forward, be bold, and be the global leader in the implementation of Indigenous rights. *UN Declaration* implementation has the potential to make an impact that transcends Indigenous peoples and Canada's borders. If this country can reshape itself so that it can accommodate Indigenous nationhood, Indigenous ontologies, and Indigenous political practices, it will become a world leader. A world that can learn to do these things successfully will be a world characterized by an entirely different set of values and power relations than has existed and continues to exist in the current international order.

NOTES

1 John F. Leslie, "The Indian Act: An Historical Perspective," *Canadian Parliamentary Review* 25, no. 2 (Summer 2002): 23–7.
2 "This Day in History: July 1, 1967," *Vancouver Sun*, July 2, 2015, http://www.vancouversun.com/This+history+July+1967/6876736/story.html.
3 Michael Bryant, "How Pierre Trudeau's Misbegotten Plan to Extinguish Indigenous Rights Ignited the Fight to Save Them," *National Post*, June 23, 2017, http://nationalpost.com/opinion/beyond-the-duck-how-pierre-trudeaus-misbegotten-plan-to-extinguish-indigenous-rights-ignited-the-fight-to-save-them.
4 *Statement of the Government of Canada on Indian Policy* (Ottawa: Queen's Printer Cat. No. R32-2469, 1969).
5 Alanis Obomsawin, *Kanehsatake: 270 Years of Resistance* (National Film Board of Canada, 1993).
6 See the major findings in Mary C. Hurley and Jill Wherrett, "The Report of the Royal Commission on Aboriginal Peoples," In Brief (Library of Parliament: Parliamentary Research Branch, 2000), http://publications.gc.ca/site/eng/299876/publication.html.
7 "The Story," Idle No More, accessed July 3, 2018, http://www.idlenomore.ca/story.
8 United Nations General Assembly, *United Nations Declaration on the Rights of Indigenous Peoples*, 2008, http://www.un.org/esa/socdev/unpfii/documents/DRIPS_en.pdf.
9 Sheryl R. Lightfoot, *Global Indigenous Politics: A Subtle Revolution*, Worlding beyond the West 8 (New York, NY: Routledge, 2016).
10 United Nations General Assembly, *United Nations Declaration on the Rights of Indigenous Peoples*.

11 Truth and Reconciliation Commission of Canada, *Final Report of the Truth and Reconciliation Commission of Canada: Honouring the Truth, Reconciling for the Future*, 2015, http://www.trc.ca/websites/trcinstitution/File/2015/Findings/Calls_to_Action_English2.pdf.

12 Liberal Party of Canada, "Truth and Reconciliation," Real Change, accessed July 3, 2018, https://www.liberal.ca/realchange/truth-and-reconciliation-2/.

13 Justin Trudeau, "Minister of Indigenous and Northern Affairs Mandate Letter," Text, November 23, 2015, https://unpublishedottawa.com/letter/31020/minister-indigenous-and-northern-affairs-mandate-letter.

14 Jody Wilson-Raybould, "Special Statement at the Opening Ceremonies of the United Nations Permanent Forum on Indigenous Issues, 15th Session" (United Nations General Assembly, New York, May 9, 2016), http://www.northernpublicaffairs.ca/index/justice-minister-jody-wilson-rayboulds-opening-address-at-un-permanent-forum-on-indigenous-issues/.

15 Tim Fontaine, "Canada Officially Adopts UN Declaration on Rights of Indigenous Peoples," *CBC News*, May 10, 2016, https://www.cbc.ca/news/indigenous/canada-adopting-implementing-un-rights-declaration-1.3575272.

16 See "Bill C-262," Canada's NDP, accessed July 3, 2018, http://romeosaganash.ndp.ca/bill-c-262.

17 John Paul Tasker, "Liberal Government Backs Bill That Demands Full Implementation of UN Indigenous Rights Declaration," *CBC News*, November 21, 2017, https://www.cbc.ca/news/politics/wilson-raybould-backs-undrip-bill-1.4412037.

18 Office of the Prime Minister of Canada, "Prime Minister Announces Working Group of Ministers on the Review of Laws and Policies Related to Indigenous Peoples," Office of the Prime Minister of Canada, February 21, 2017, https://pm.gc.ca/eng/news/2017/02/22/prime-minister-announces-working-group-ministers-review-laws-and-policies-related.

19 Department of Justice, "Principles Respecting the Government of Canada's Relationship with Indigenous Peoples," July 14, 2017, http://www.justice.gc.ca/eng/csj-sjc/principles-principes.html.

20 "Indigenous Leaders at UN Headquarters to Discuss Landmark Rights Declaration," *CBC News*, April 24, 2017, https://www.cbc.ca/news/indigenous/undrip-one-year-since-implementing-1.4083450.

21 Office of the Prime Minister of Canada, "Statement by the Prime Minister of Canada on Changes to the Ministry," Prime Minister of Canada, August 28, 2017, https://pm.gc.ca/eng/news/2017/08/28/statement-prime-minister-canada-changes-ministry.

15 Reconciliation with a Question Mark: Three Moments

CHRISTA SCHOLTZ

The question facing Canada at and after its sesquicentennial is how to achieve a just reconciliation between Indigenous peoples and the political community of Canada. I think there are two views on reconciliation: one sees us on the path towards it, awkwardly yet not devoid of grace; and another sees Canada continuing on the same old path with no reconciliation at its end, esthetics in movement notwithstanding. We need not assume that anyone who holds either view is acting in bad faith. Both may be acting sincerely according to their definitions of what reconciliation is and what it requires. But if that is true, then they hold different definitions.

I use this definition of reconciliation: the act of making one thing compatible with another. Reconciliation in this basic sense is about resolving two things understood to be in conflict. The definition says precisely nothing about the nature of the conflict or its potential resolution. Reconciliation is silent on whether A moves towards B's position where B holds firm, whether B moves towards A's position where A holds firm, or whether both A and B move to meet somewhere in the middle in a pattern of mutual adjustment. The story of mutual adjustment is intuitively pleasing: both parties unsettle themselves to some degree in order to achieve moderation and signal mutual regard. Underlying this intuition is the pleasing assumption that justice lies somewhere between them. How are we to think about the scenarios where adjustment is unidirectional? This also depends on where we assume justice lies. If B holds the just position, then A *should* unsettle itself. Any movement by B towards A would decrease conflict, and hence move toward reconciliation – but at the steep cost of justice. In the simplest case, A and B have a shared understanding of where justice lies, and the main challenge is to agree on what terms or what actions will move either or both toward that shared point. The more fraught scenario is when there is no agreed-upon point on which to coordinate, and the primary challenge is a political and philosophical struggle over the end point itself.

In this paper, I show how Canada has historically understood reconciliation between itself and Indigenous peoples. I also pay attention to Canada's assumptions about where justice lies. I engage with three moments: one after Confederation, centred on the 1876 Indian Act; another in 1969, when the Trudeau White Paper on Indian Affairs was introduced; and a third moment with the entrenchment of Aboriginal and treaty rights, under the Constitution Act, 1982.

Moment 1: The Indian Act, 1876

Early in Confederation, Parliament set out its understanding of the conflict between itself and Indigenous peoples in the 1876 Indian Act. The Act operationalized a binary that distinguished Indians as a legal category of persons separate from the Canadian political community. Once so defined, Parliament subjected Indians to conditions and controls that burdened no other. Indians were held apart legally and spatially (through the reserve lands provisions), but the legislation also foresaw the possibility that this separation could end. Parliament established a pathway for Indians to be made compatible with other Canadians. The pathway's procedures made clear that the conflict between Indians and others was about civilization, where the Indian's assumed state was incivility. An Indian could join the ranks of Canadians only once he satisfied the government that the default no longer applied. He could demonstrate this through higher learning, by practising the medical or legal professions, being ordained by a Christian denomination, or by entering Holy Orders.[1] Absent this learning, the Indian could make an application and invite the government's review of "the degree of civilization to which he or she has attained, and the character for integrity, morality, and sobriety which he or she bears."[2] Once so approved, the Indian would achieve the status of a "probationary Indian," and after a subsequent period of at least three years, be finally relieved of Indian status. Mindful of achieving certain administrative efficiencies, Parliament offered a similar pathway to bands of Indians.[3]

As told through this 1876 Act, Parliament clearly understood its position to be just, and inflicted no burden on itself, or on Canadians generally, to change in order to achieve a compatibility with the Indians in their midst. The statute betrayed no doubts about the wisdom of Canada's vision for the way forward. The burdens of this reconciliation lay squarely on the Indians, who must correct their perceived deficiencies in order to be accepted as members of Canada's political community. While the legislation foresaw the possibility of reconciliation should Indians successfully undertake those burdens, it also prepared for a future where the conflict persists. Parliament's expectation was that the future involved fewer Indians, but allowed Indians to retain their old "uncivil" ways, thereby willfully rejecting Canada's conditional embrace.

The voluntarism of the 1876 Indian Act did not last very long. With the Indians' resistance to the reconciliation on offer, Parliament amended it to incorporate a more coercive approach towards the Indian problem. Parliament widened the discretion of its agents to remove Indians' status unilaterally. Parliament initially allowed its agents the discretion to decide whether Indian children's attendance in residential school was compulsory or not, but then removed this discretion in the 1920s. Parliament's reconciliation project involved the forced removal of generations of Indian children from their families to residential schools. The project of making Indians compatible with Canada's understanding of itself exacted a steep price, one that continues to be paid.

Moment 2: The Statement on Indian Policy, 1969

Just after Canada marked its centennial, Pierre Trudeau's (in)famous White Paper told another reconciliation story. It did not begin on a clean page. Ninety-three years of the Indian Act made it impossible to start anew. Trudeau's reconciliation project shared important goals with 1876, and yet also departed from it. The White Paper's key departure from 1876 was its rejection of civilization discourse. The Indian was no longer Canada's uncivilized foil. The Indian was no longer cast as deficient, her heritage no longer anathema to Canada's civil project. Instead, "Canada is richer for its Indian component, although there have been times when diversity seemed of little value to many Canadians."[4] Instead, Indians must be "... free to develop Indian cultures in an environment of legal, social, and economic equality with other Canadians."[5] Canadians were reminded that "... cultural heritage [is] a source of personal strength" for Indians like all others.[6] The Indian who held onto culture, and history, and language, despite all the carnage wrought by Canadian Indian policy, was no longer barred from the Canadian political community. Indians were to take their place in Canada's growing cultural pluralism. The paper recognized that Canada had a concomitant responsibility to be welcoming, to "recognize the need for changed attitudes and a truly open society."[7]

But as this is a reconciliation story, there must by my definition be an incompatibility between Indians and Canadians that needed to be resolved. The White Paper framed this incompatibility as one of legal, rather than cultural, difference. Legal difference between Indian and non-Indian had led to discriminatory treatment, with ruinous policy effects that have left Indians unfree, apart, on the margins. The problem was that Indians had a special legal status from other Canadians, and this is what Canada had to resolve. This required the de-Indianizing of the Constitution, hence ridding the British North America Act of Section 91(24), repealing the Indian Act, and, eventually, "equitably end[ing]" the historic treaties.[8] It required the transfer of reserve lands to Indians as fee simple lands. The result was the end of Indians as peoples to whom Canada had distinct legal obligations.

But where the burdens of the 1876 project rested uniquely on Indians' shoulders, in 1969 the burdens of reconciliation were shared in some sense and involved a kind of reciprocity that was utterly absent in the earlier Act. Canada had to change its constitution, revise its laws, update its attitudes, open its embrace. Canada had to make some adjustments in order to expect Indians to make their own. If Canada transferred reserve lands to Indian control, then Indians were to pay taxes on that land. If Canada ended discrimination, then Indians were no longer to expect special treatment in government services. If Canada appointed a claims commissioner to address historical grievances, then Indians should move beyond the past.

We know that Canada's First Nations soundly rejected the White Paper's reconciliation proposal. Canada's new openness and positive valuation of their cultural heritage could never outweigh Canada's rejection of the treaties, their legal interests, their status as self-determining communities. First Nations, Inuit, and Métis mobilized and fought for the patriated Canadian constitution to entrench the legal rights the White Paper sought to deny.

Moment 3: Constitution Act, 1982

Thirteen years after the White Paper, Section 35 of the Constitution Act, 1982 announced that the "[t]he existing aboriginal and treaty rights of the aboriginal peoples of Canada are hereby recognized and affirmed."

The value of the words was unclear in 1982, but the promise was large. If constitutional recognition and affirmation meant anything, Aboriginal and treaty rights now limited the scope of government authority to act within its jurisdiction. The constitutional commitment was itself revocable. But barring a formal amendment, it is here to stay. The question is whether we live up to its promise.

This reconciliation story is different from the two I have already set out, for at least three reasons. The first is that Section 35 foresees a future where Indigenous peoples and their rights do not disappear. The second is that unlike a statute and a formal government policy paper, the judicial branch has been the primary state narrator of Section 35. This is not to say that legislative chambers, the executive, and Indigenous peoples are silent in Section 35's story. Rather, the courts have a large, perhaps outsized, role in how the story is shaped. The third is that the Supreme Court has explicitly used the word "reconciliation" to tell it. The word is constantly present, but what the Court reconciles with what changes over time. I cannot provide a comprehensive account of the Court's jurisprudence here, but I can provide a few snapshots.

From the beginning, the Court understood that this constitutional commitment needed to "import some constraint on the exercise of sovereign power."[9] The conflict to be resolved was internal to the Sovereign: "federal power must be reconciled with federal duty and the best way to achieve that reconciliation is to demand justification of any government regulation that infringes upon or denies aboriginal rights."[10] In this inward-facing formulation, the Sovereign reconciles itself with what it means to be a good Sovereign with respect to Aboriginal rights. It can still limit or deny these rights, but only to the extent necessary, and only for very good reason.

The formulation becomes more outward-facing in subsequent cases. The conflict to be resolved becomes about what lies between the Crown and Indigenous peoples. When the Court first defined an Aboriginal right, it identified the purpose of Section 35 as reconciling the "sovereignty of the Crown" with "the fact that aboriginals lived on the land in distinctive societies, with their own practices, traditions and cultures."[11] This reconciliatory purpose requires Canada protect integral Aboriginal practices rooted in the past, while limiting the contemporary definition of those practices so that they are cognizable to Canada's legal system. The Court writes: "The only fair and just reconciliation is ... one which takes into account the aboriginal perspective while at the same time taking into account the perspective of the common law. True reconciliation will, equally, place weight on each."[12] The Court views reconciliation here as an equally shared burden wherein a restrictive definition of Aboriginal rights balances the limitations placed on the Crown's power. The counterview is that the burden is not at all equal, as Aboriginal rights are defined away precisely when they would otherwise present a real challenge to Canada's legal system. The charge is that the Canadian legal system elides the epistemic responsibility that comes when truly engaging with Indigenous difference.

More recently, the Court has moved towards understanding reconciliation as born out of a negotiated political process. The Court recognizes a conflict between the Crown's and Indigenous peoples' sovereignty assertions, and that a political process is the chief mechanism to mediating the conflict. For instance: "Treaties serve to reconcile pre-existing Aboriginal sovereignty with assumed Crown sovereignty ... sovereignty claims [are] reconciled through the process of honourable negotiation."[13] And in the last few months: "As expressions of partnership between nations, modern treaties play a critical role in fostering reconciliation ... Negotiating modern treaties, and living by the mutual rights and responsibilities they set out, has the potential to forge a renewed relationship between the Crown and Indigenous peoples."[14]

Conclusion

By placing the modern treaty process at the centre of the reconciliation story, the Supreme Court has recognized its inability to provide a lasting reconciliation on its own. The courts have made decisions that have shifted Indigenous political bargaining power, but Indigenous peoples and the Crown do not bargain on equal terms. There is no Indigenous veto over state action. The Crown can limit the treaty rights for which Indigenous peoples would have made concessions to obtain. Indigenous peoples are called upon to adjust their positions to make them more compatible with the Crown. In the story of Section 35 so far, Canada is not unsettled in a truly significant way, even if one considers the path that we are on now to be moving, even inelegantly, towards justice. But for those who believe that justice requires Indigenous peoples to hold firm and for Canada to adjust, this reconciliation story sounds like a promise unfulfilled.

Reconciliation in our time is a tricky proposition. While the Truth and Reconciliation Commission (2008–2015) has increased the public salience of a reconciliation discourse, it has also highlighted the different ways in which the concept remains contested. We must look beyond the mere use of the word to reach a conclusion about whether the reconciliation on offer is actually just. I think it fair to say that Canada at 150 years is doing a better job than at 9, but I also think it important to highlight that the modern reconciliation process remains problematic. As it has always been, the future will be a political struggle over what justice requires, and who should bear the burdens of making our future compatible with it.

NOTES

1   *An Act to amend and consolidate the laws respecting Indians*, S.C. 1876, c.18, s.86(1).
2   *An Act to amend and consolidate*, s.86(1).
3   *An Act to amend and consolidate*, s.93.
4   *Statement of the Government of Canada on Indian Policy* (Ottawa: Queen's Printer Cat. No. R32-2469, 1969), 3.
5   *Statement of the Government of Canada*, 3.
6   *Statement of the Government of Canada*, 8.
7   *Statement of the Government of Canada*, 5.
8   *Statement of the Government of Canada*, 11.
9   *R. v. Sparrow*, [1990] 1 S.C.R. 1075, para. 1109.
10   *R. v. Sparrow*, para. 1109.
11   *R. v. Van der Peet*, [1996] 2 S.C.R. 507, para. 31.
12   *R. v. Van der Peet*, para. 50.
13   *Haida Nation v. British Columbia*, [2004] 3 S.C.R. 511, para. 20.
14   *First Nation of Nacho Nyak Dun v. Yukon*, [2017] SCC 58, para. 1.

16 Reconciliation, Colonization, and Climate Futures

DEBORAH MCGREGOR

Indigenous peoples, often among the world's most marginalized and impoverished peoples, will bear the brunt of the catastrophe of climate change.[1]

To the Commission, reconciliation is about establishing and maintaining a mutually respectful relationship between Aboriginal and non-Aboriginal peoples in this country. In order for that to happen, there has to be awareness of the past, acknowledgement of the harm that has been incited, atonement for the causes, and action to change behaviour.[2]

It is my argument that any climate change policy that is put forward internationally (Paris Climate Agreement), nationally (Pan-Canadian Framework on Clean Growth and Climate Change), or provincially (Ontario's Climate Change Action Plan) must consider the rights and interests of Indigenous peoples as well as historical and ongoing processes of colonization. It is recognized, internationally and in Canada, that Indigenous peoples are more vulnerable to the impacts of climate change than other peoples due to distinct connections to the natural world.[3] As noted in the above quote, due to historical imperial and colonializing forces, Indigenous peoples "are among the poorest of the poor, and thus the most threatened segment of the world's population in terms of social, economic, and environmental vulnerability."[4] In Canada, the situation is similar, as Indigenous peoples are confronted with disparities and disadvantages in every conceivable indicator of well-being.[5] Climate change will exacerbate these challenges as Indigenous peoples continue to seek justice in their relationships with dominant, broader society.

Recently, Assembly of First Nations regional chief Bill Erasmus emphasized in regards to climate change the vital need to

> ... respect and take into account traditional knowledge when scientific measures are being used, recognize Indigenous Peoples' authority in their own homelands and territories when it comes to climate change. Including recognition of Indigenous rights on climate change initiatives is crucial, said Erasmus, because Indigenous Peoples tend to be the most vulnerable to the rapidly-changing climate. *We are most hit by what happens immediately to the land.*[6]

In Canada, key policy initiatives regarding Indigenous peoples have arisen over the past fifty years from the following undertakings:

- the Hawthorne report (1966–67);
- the *Statement of the Government of Canada on Indian Policy* (commonly referred to as the 1969 "White Paper");
- the Royal Commission on Aboriginal Peoples (1996);
- the Ipperwash Inquiry (2007);
- the Truth and Reconciliation Commission (2015); and
- the *United Nations Declaration on the Rights of Indigenous Peoples* (UNDRIP) adoption by the Government of Canada in 2016.

As is discussed below, the earlier of these policy initiatives focused on continuing the process of colonization, i.e., "getting rid of the Indian,"[7] so that dominant Canadian society could have unfettered access to the lands and resources encompassed by the traditional territories of Indigenous peoples. While the more recent initiatives have begun to expose the injustice of this approach, no policy, either climate-based or otherwise, is going to be successful in the long run if it does not result in genuine restructuring and transformation of contemporary relationships between the state and Indigenous peoples.

It is for this reason that I suggest that current climate policy in Canada does not address in any substantial way the concerns and interests of Indigenous peoples. Canadian government policy continues to undermine Indigenous peoples in terms of sovereignty, authority, jurisdiction, and application of Indigenous laws in relation to the land. This has not changed substantially over the past fifty (and more) years, nor does it look set to do so over the next fifty years. Again, the underlying challenge comes down to the centuries-old conflict around control over land.[8] Colonial and later Canadian policies, laws, and practices have denied Indigenous peoples sovereignty over their lands, and the climate change agenda has not sought to resolve this issue. Canada continues to rely on the exploitation of Indigenous lands and resources in order to advance its own national interests.

The Last Fifty Years of Indigenous Public Policy

In 2017, exactly 150 years after Confederation, we see clearly that "Land" remains central to the prosperity of Canada. This same land has been under Indigenous authority and jurisdiction since time immemorial. To obtain the lands of Indigenous peoples, colonial and later Canadian governments sought to "get rid of" Indigenous peoples from the lands they inhabit.[9] A variety of strategies has aimed directly or indirectly at achieving this, including undermining and eradicating traditional systems of government, as well as actually dispossessing Indigenous nations of their lands and territories. The Truth and Reconciliation Commission found that:

> The Canadian government pursued this policy of cultural genocide because it wished to divest itself of its legal and financial obligations to Aboriginal people and gain control over their land and resources. If every Aboriginal person were "absorbed into the body politic," there would be no reserves, no Treaties, and no Aboriginal rights.[10]

By 1967, this logic was already firmly entrenched through well-established laws, agreements, policies, and practices. In the 1960s, discourse on human rights began to influence public policy, and in response, Canada commissioned anthropologist Harry Hawthorn to conduct a comprehensive national study of the situation of "Indians" in Canada in 1963. Hawthorn released two volumes of his study, one in 1966 and the other a year later, under the title *A Survey of the Contemporary Indians of Canada: Economic, Political, Educational Needs, and Policies*. A century after Confederation, many Canadians thus learned for the first time of the appalling conditions in which Indigenous peoples across Canada were forced to live. The study offered hundreds of recommendations for improvement, particularly in the areas of health and education. Despite this, however, its principal focus remained true to the overriding government policy of assimilation.[11]

In 1969, Prime Minister Pierre Elliott Trudeau, through the *Statement of the Government of Canada on Indian Policy* (commonly referred to as the "White Paper"), again put forth an aggressive assimilation policy to eliminate the Indians, their lands, and treaties. The stated intention of the policy was "the remaking of Indians into 'Canadians as all other Canadians.'"[12] Widely opposed by Indigenous peoples, this particular policy was eventually abandoned, yet the conflicts over sovereignty and lands persist.

Established in 1991, the Royal Commission on Aboriginal Peoples (RCAP) released its final report and concluded in no uncertain terms that *"The main policy direction, pursued for more than 150 years, first by colonial then by Canadian governments, has been wrong."*[13] RCAP called for a fundamental change in the social and political order of Indigenous/ non-Indigenous relations, namely the revitalization of coexistence and "Nation-to-Nation" relationships. Over 400 recommendations were presented to assist in making this change a reality, the majority of which unfortunately remain unaddressed.

The 2007 Ipperwash Inquiry explicitly recognized the importance of land to Indigenous peoples:

> The immediate catalyst for major occupations and protests is a dispute over a land claim, a burial site, resource development, or harvesting, hunting, and fishing rights. The fundamental conflict, however, is *usually about land*. Contemporary Aboriginal occupations and conflicts should therefore be seen as part of the centuries-old tension between Aboriginal Peoples and non-Aboriginal people over the control, use and ownership of land.[14]

Nearly two decades later, the 2015 Report of the Truth and Reconciliation Commission (TRC) revealed similar findings. The TRC confirms that the basis for the acrimonious nature of the relationship between Indigenous and non-Indigenous peoples has been the goal of the Canadian State to eradicate Indigenous peoples in order to obtain their lands.

RCAP, the TRC, and UNDRIP have all called for a reckoning with this past and a move towards a future of reconciliation, coexistence, and self-determination. As a further step towards this, the Government of Canada committed to fully supporting UNDRIP and implementing its provisions.[15] This is a position consistent with the "Calls to Action" outlined by the TRC, and is explicitly stated as its "Principle One," which reads: "The *United Nations Declaration on the Rights of Indigenous Peoples* is the framework for reconciliation at all levels and across all sectors of Canadian society."[16] In 2017, the Government of Canada released the *Principles Respecting the Government of Canada's Relationships with Indigenous Peoples*, which outlines ten principles to guide the development of "renewed relationship."[17]

Whatever the case, the fact remains that if environmental and/or climate policy does not address the fact that the interests and concerns of Indigenous peoples are rooted in a colonial history, they risk further entrenching an ongoing colonial legacy that alienates Indigenous peoples from their lands and livelihood. Within this situation then, what can reconciliation offer as it is conceptualized by Indigenous peoples?

The Role of Reconciliation

The TRC defines "reconciliation" as:

> ... an ongoing process of establishing and maintaining respectful relationships. A critical part of this process involves repairing damaged trust by making apologies, providing individual and collective reparations, and following through with concrete actions that demonstrate real societal change. Establishing respectful relationships also requires the revitalization of Indigenous law and legal traditions.[18]

Reconciliation must be an ongoing process, because as John Borrows declares, "Colonialism is not only a historic practice, it continues to be acted upon and reinvented in old and new forms to the detriment of Indigenous Peoples."[19] Furthermore, it will be critically important to privilege Indigenous conceptions of reconciliation based on Indigenous legal traditions, knowledges, protocols, and practices. It is not appropriate to rely on state-conceived and sponsored frameworks of reconciliation as these processes may well be to our collective detriment. This is particularly true as such processes do not adequately address the land issue, nor do they reflect Indigenous concepts of reconciliation, which see the land/natural world as critical agents in any meaningful reconciliation undertaking. Concepts of reconciliation, especially if they are to be applied to environmental policy, must be expanded upon to reflect Indigenous peoples' understanding. Reconciliation applies not only to reconciliation between peoples. As Mi'kmaq Elder Stephen Augustine suggests, "Other dimensions of human experience – our relationships with the earth and all living beings – are also relevant in working towards reconciliation."[20] These sentiments are also captured in the words shared by Elder Reg Crowshoe as he explains:

> Reconciliation requires talking, but our conversations must be broader than Canada's conventional approaches. Reconciliation between Aboriginal and non-Aboriginal Canadians, from an Aboriginal perspective, also *requires Reconciliation with the natural world. If human beings resolve problems between themselves but continue to destroy the natural world, then reconciliation remains incomplete.*[21]

In other words, we must reconcile with the Earth, not just with each other, or reconciliation remains incomplete and our collective future uncertain. These concepts then become the criteria (or tests) for whether environmental and climate policies will actually resolve the challenges they seek to address.

Reconciliation, Environment, and Climate Change: Future Challenges

> Reconciliation must support Aboriginal peoples as they heal from the destructive legacies of colonization that have wreaked such havoc in their lives. But it must do even more. Reconciliation must inspire Aboriginal and non-Aboriginal peoples to transform Canadian society so that our children and grandchildren can live together in dignity, peace, and prosperity on these lands we now share.[22]

Reconciliation has not been identified as an outcome of environmental or climate change policy in Canada – yet it should be! Reconciliation based on Indigenous legal traditions, governance, and knowledge systems offers an alternative to environmental regulatory reform currently under review by the Government of Canada.[23] It also seeks to explicitly address ongoing colonialism in order to move to a just future that includes not only peace between peoples, but with the natural world as well. Conceptions of reconciliation in climate and environmental policy and regulatory regimes must:

1 Recognize and address ongoing colonialism that continues to alienate Indigenous peoples from their lands/waters and creates the conditions for climate change vulnerability;

2 Extend the conceptions of reconciliation to include the natural world; and

3 Engage with Indigenous legal and intellectual traditions to derive environmental/climate change policy/approaches.

As the TRC asserts, "Aboriginal peoples' cultural revitalization and integrating Indigenous knowledge systems, oral histories, laws, protocols, and connections to the land into the reconciliation process are essential."[24] To the extent that Canadian reconciliation policies fail to incorporate these essential components, they will continue to fail Indigenous peoples and the natural world. To date, the outcomes of the environmental review process and current climate policies (at all levels in Canada) are disappointing in this regard.[25]

Indigenous conceptions of reconciliation based on Indigenous legal systems and knowledge have much to offer the future sustainability of Canada and should be given the utmost respect in environmental and climate deliberations. Reconciliation, if it is to achieve its stated goals, must not only be concerned with healing relationships among peoples, but also with the land itself, and must occur at a societal level to be truly transformative and secure a sustainable future.[26]

NOTES

1 Inter-Agency Support Group on Indigenous Peoples' Issues, *Collated Paper on Indigenous Peoples and Climate Change* (New York: United Nations Economic and Social Council, 2008). http://www.un.org/esa/socdev/unpfii/documents/2016/egm/IASG-Collated-Paper-on-Indigenous-Peoples-and-Climate-Change.pdf.

2 Truth and Reconciliation Commission of Canada, *Final Report of the Truth and Reconciliation Commission of Canada: Honouring the Truth, Reconciling for the Future*, 2015, 6, http://www.trc.ca/websites/trcinstitution/File/2015/Findings/Calls_to_Action_English2.pdf.

3 Center for Indigenous Environmental Resources, *How Climate Change Uniquely Impacts the Social, Physical, and Cultural Aspects of First Nations. Report Prepared for the Assembly of the First Nations.* http://www.afn.ca/uploads/files/env/report_2_cc_uniquely_impacts_physical_social_and_cultural_aspects_final_001.pdf.

4 International Labour Organization, *Indigenous People and Climate Change* (Geneva: International Labour Office, 2017), ix. http://www.ilo.org/

wcmsp5/groups/public/---dgreports/---gender/documents/publication/
wcms_551189.pdf.

5 James Anaya, *The Situation of Indigenous Peoples in Canada. Report of
the Special Rapporteur on the Rights of Indigenous Peoples* (New York:
United Nations General Assembly, 2014). http://unsr.jamesanaya.org/
country-reports/the-situation-of-indigenous-peoples-in-canada.

6 Brandi Morin, "Assembly of First Nations to Have Seat at International
Climate Change Conference for First Time," *CBC News*, November 4, 2017,
http://www.cbc.ca/news/indigenous/afn-climate-change-germany-
1.4387206.

7 John L. Tobias, "Protection, Civilization, Assimilation: An Outline
History of Canada's Indian Policy," in *Sweet Promises: A Reader on
Indian-White Relations in Canada*, ed. J.R. Miller (University of Toronto
Press, 1991), 127–44.

8 Sidney B. Linden, *Report of the Ipperwash Inquiry*, vol. 2 (Ontario, 2007),
https://www.attorneygeneral.jus.gov.on.ca/inquiries/ipperwash/index.
html.

9 Tobias, "Protection, Civilization, Assimilation: An Outline History of
Canada's Indian Policy."

10 Murray Sinclair, Marie Wilson, and Chief Wilton Littlechild, *What We
Have Learned: Principles of Truth and Reconciliation*, 2015, 3, http://www.trc.
ca/websites/trcinstitution/File/2015/Findings/Principles_2015_05_31_
web_o.pdf.

11 James Frideres and Lilianne E. Krosenbrink-Gelissen, *Native Peoples in
Canada: Contemporary Conflicts* (Prentice-Hall Canada, 1993).

12 Menno Boldt, *Surviving as Indians: The Challenge of Self-Government* (Toronto:
University of Toronto Press, 1993), 18.

13 Royal Commission on Aboriginal Peoples, *People to People, Nation to Nation:
Highlights from the Report of the Royal Commission on Aboriginal Peoples* (Ottawa:
Minister of Supply and Services Canada, 1996), 1.

14 Linden, *Report of the Ipperwash Inquiry*, 2:15.

15 Tim Fontaine, 2016 1:16 PM ET | Last Updated: August 2, and 2016,
"Canada Now Full Supporter of UN Indigenous Rights Declaration,"
CBC News, May 10, 2016, http://www.cbc.ca/news/indigenous/
canada-adopting-implementing-un-rights-declaration-1.3575272.

16 Truth and Reconciliation Commission of Canada, *Final Report of the Truth
and Reconciliation Commission of Canada*, 4.

17 *Principles Respecting the Government of Canada's Relationships with Indigenous
Peoples* (Ottawa: Department of Justice, 2017), 1.

18 Sinclair, Wilson, and Littlechild, *What We Have Learned*, 121.

19 John Borrows, *Freedom and Indigenous Constitutionalism* (Toronto: University of Toronto Press, 2016).

20 Sinclair, Wilson, and Littlechild, *What We Have Learned*, 122.

21 Sinclair, Wilson, and Littlechild, 123.

22 Truth and Reconciliation Commission of Canada, *Final Report of the Truth and Reconciliation Commission of Canada*, 8.

23 *Environmental and Regulatory Reviews* (Ottawa: Government of Canada, 2017); *Review of Environmental and Regulatory Processes* (Ottawa: Government of Canada, 2018). https://www.canada.ca/en/services/environment/.

24 Sinclair, Wilson, and Littlechild, *What We Have Learned*, 4.

25 *Environmental and Regulatory Reviews*.

26 Lorelei A. Lambert, *Research for Indigenous Survival: Indigenous Research Methodologies in the Behavioral Sciences* (Pablo, Montana: Salish Kootenai College Press, distributed by University of Nebraska Press, 2014).

PART FOUR

Canada's Borders and Beyond

17 Fifty Years of Canadian Immigration Policy[1]

ANTJE ELLERMANN

It has been fifty years since Canada took the historic step of abolishing race-based immigrant admissions. The 1967 immigration regulations removed any remaining ethnoracial discrimination from family sponsorship and placed economic immigration policy on a skills-based footing. A decade later, the 1976 Immigration Act institutionalized these changes and broke new ground by articulating the fundamental principles governing Canadian immigration policy. The Act, which remains the cornerstone of present-day immigration policy, established three distinct immigration streams, each serving a distinct goal. First, family sponsorship was "to facilitate the reunion in Canada of Canadian citizens and permanent residents with their close relatives from abroad." Second, economic immigration was to select skilled workers and business immigrants who would "foster the development of a strong and viable economy and the prosperity of all regions in Canada." Third, humanitarian immigration was "to fulfil Canada's international legal obligations with respect to refugees and to uphold its humanitarian tradition with respect to the displaced and the persecuted."[2] The policy goals of each stream – family reunification, economic growth, and refugee protection – continue to enjoy broad societal and bipartisan support today. Thus, in this appraisal of the past fifty years of Canadian immigration policy we ask, to what extent has Canada succeeded in achieving these goals?

Canada's Commitment to Family Reunification

With the passage of the 1976 Immigration Act, Canadian lawmakers turned their back on race-based family admissions and embraced the universal sponsorship of spouses, children, parents, and grandparents of Canadian citizens and permanent residents. Thus, the Act cemented family reunification in terms of the recognition of human interdependence regardless of race and ethnicity, at least within the confines of Western understandings of family relations: "When Canada accepts immigrants, we consider ourselves duty-bound also to accept those close relatives who would normally be dependent on them in a society such as our own."[3] Looking back at the past five decades of family immigration, then, how well has Canada lived up to its commitment "to alleviate, never to exacerbate" the involuntary separation of families?[4]

When it comes to the sponsorship of immediate family members – spouses and dependent children – Canada has lived up to its commitment to unifying transnational families by progressively expanding the circle of those eligible for sponsorship. The 2002 Immigration and Refugee Protection Act formally abolished heterosexism in family admissions by extending spousal sponsorship rights to common-law and same-sex partners.[5] Lawmakers further ended the differential treatment of families with disabilities by exempting sponsored spouses and dependent children from medical inadmissibly provisions that would otherwise preclude admission to Canada.[6] Thus, just as the 1976 Act institutionalized the elimination of race-based discrimination in family admissions, the 2001 Act removed discrimination based on sexual orientation and disability.[7]

Although the admission of immediate family members has been marked by liberalization, access to the sponsorship of parents and grandparents has become increasingly curtailed. Starting in the early 1990s, parent and grandparent visas were slashed in an attempt to tilt the balance of immigrant admissions from the family stream to the economic stream. By 2011, parent and grandparent visas had fallen from 41,000 in 1994 to 14,000, with wait times of up to six years. This trend was aggravated in 2012. After imposing a two-year program moratorium, the Harper government set admission levels at a historic low of 5,000 while increasing the minimum income threshold by 30 per cent and doubling the length of sponsorship obligations to 20 years. In principle, those parents and grandparents excluded from sponsorship could apply for the new temporary super visa. However, its stringent income and health insurance conditions pushed it out of reach for many families. Most importantly, the super visa was not designed as a substitution for family sponsorship as it treats visa holders as visitors, rather than immigrants. While the Trudeau government's decision to increase parent and grandparent visas to 20,000 by 2018 marks an important policy correction, it would be erroneous to conceive it as a period of generous family reunification – it is merely a return to the pre-2012 status quo.

The progressive shrinking of access to family unification for parents and grandparents is a reflection of the ideational spillover of neoliberal arguments into a policy area that, since the 1976 Act, has traditionally been normatively grounded in the protection of family unity. To quote Conservative Citizenship and Immigration Minister Jason Kenney in 2013: "If you think your parents may need to go on welfare in Canada, please don't sponsor them. We're not looking for more people on welfare, we're not looking to add people as a social burden to Canada."[8] As elderly relatives have become construed as burdens on Canadian society, policymakers have lost sight of the emotional and material importance of intergenerational care. For many families, being denied access to parent or grandparent sponsorship means that they are unable to provide care for their aging parents. Parents and grandparents, on the other hand, are denied the opportunity to offer childcare and household support to their financially- and time-stretched families in Canada. Ironically, given the cost of childcare in Canada, the families who are least able to afford sponsorship of elderly relatives are the ones who are most likely to materially benefit from it.

If Canada is to remain serious about facilitating the reunification of families, policymakers need to stop further entrenching existing socioeconomic inequalities and put an end to sponsorship rules that place access to parent and grandparent sponsorship out of reach for many. Demand for the sponsorship of elderly relatives is not going to disappear. On the contrary, instead of treating intergenerational dependence as a problem to be erased, we need to embrace it as an expression of our shared humanity. Parents and grandparents are not tourists, nor should their ability to live with their families remain a privilege of the materially and economically able. Instead of viewing family sponsorship through the narrow and inhumane lens of economic utility, Canada needs to return to the ethics of care that informed the establishment of its family sponsorship system in the first place.

Canada's Commitment to Merit-based Immigration

With the creation of the point system in 1967, Canada placed economic immigration on a skills-based footing. From now on, as Minister of Immigration and Citizenship Ellen Fairclough declared, "any suitably qualified person from any part of the world can be considered for immigration to Canada entirely on his own merits without regard to his race, colour, national origin, or the country from which he comes."[9]

Until the early 1990s, the notion of "skill" was largely used in juxtaposition to "race" to describe a non-discriminatory immigration policy that was based on occupational qualification, rather than national origin. Point system admissions were coupled to the state of the economy and favoured applicants from in-demand occupations. Starting in the 1990s, reforms to the point system shifted the logic of economic admissions from occupational demand to human capital. Human capital-based admissions are premised on a highly selective notion of skill – namely attributes associated with the global knowledge economy such as advanced formal education, language capacity, and financial assets. With the passage of the Immigration and Refugee Protection Act in 2001, "skill" as the basis of immigrant selection came to take on the meaning of "highly skilled."

As the skills profile of Canada's economic stream shifted upward, however, low-skilled sectors became more vulnerable to labor shortages. Starting in the mid-1990s, temporary foreign worker admissions, which were dominated by low-skilled workers, started to rise steeply, a trend that accelerated with the Conservatives' coming to power in 2006. By 2008, in a historically unprecedented development, temporary foreign worker admissions surpassed not only economic stream admissions, but all three permanent streams – economic, family, and humanitarian – streams combined. Hence, for the first time in Canadian history, more foreign nationals were admitted as temporary workers than as permanent residents. In a second consequential development, Canada's preference for highly-skilled, highly-educated, and wealthy economic immigrants had significant spillover effects on the treatment of temporary foreign workers. With few exceptions, Canada's enormous temporary foreign worker population is bifurcated.[10] On the one hand, there is a small proportion of highly-skilled workers who arrive on temporary visas and are later given access to permanent residence and family unification. On the other, there are workers in low-skilled sectors that are given access to neither. The increasing significance of "two-step immigration" programs that provide skilled temporary foreign workers with a gateway to permanent residence – such as the Canadian Experience Class and the Provincial Nominee Program – have put Canada's traditional "one-step immigration" model under attack. Whereas in 2000 close to 90 per cent of all economic stream arrivals were one-step immigration admissions through the Federal Skilled Worker program, by 2015 – as a result of the pervasiveness of two-step immigration via the Canadian Experience Class and the Provincial Nominee Programs – only about 40 per cent of economic stream admissions were "one-step immigrants."

The patterns described here are deeply problematic. Canada's heavy reliance on temporary foreign workers presents a threat to Canada's comparative success in accepting and integrating high numbers of newcomers without jeopardizing public support. The admission of temporary foreign workers not only enjoys significantly less popularity, but also risks the exploitation of workers, wage dumping, and the growth of a sizeable population of undocumented immigrants. Moreover, those temporary foreign workers who eventually succeed in becoming permanent residents do so without access to Canada's extensive network of settlement and integration services.

Temporary foreign worker recruitment can be morally justified if it fills short-term labour shortages. However, the sustained mass recruitment of temporary foreign workers of the past twenty years indicates that supposedly temporary labour needs in these sectors have become a structural part of the Canadian economy. Moreover, the hierarchization of economic migrants' access to permanent residence that has accompanied the expansion of temporary foreign worker recruitment in Canada devalues the economic contributions of low-skilled foreign workers, belying the fact that competitive knowledge economies, such as ours, are existentially dependent on their contributions. With the immigration reforms of the 1960s, economic immigration to Canada came to be premised on the notion of "merit" – economic immigrants were to be admitted as future citizens on the basis of occupational and professional skills that would contribute to Canada's economic growth. If we are to continue to base economic admissions on the notion of merit, and given our understanding of merit as the skills and labour that foreign workers contribute to our economy, then any worker recruited on the basis of skill – whether low- or high-skilled – deserves to be offered the opportunity to settle in Canada.

Canada's Commitment to Humanitarianism

The 1976 Act was the first Canadian immigration legislation to recognize refugees as a distinct class of immigrants. It legally entrenched the definition of a Convention refugee, provided for humanitarian admissions, created a refugee determination system, and enabled the private sponsorship of refugees.[11] Since then, Canada has resettled more than half a million refugees from abroad. The United Nations High Commissioner for Refugees publicly honoured Canada's commitment to refugee protection in 1986 by awarding the Nansen medal to the People of Canada "in recognition of their essential and constant contribution to the cause of refugees." It has been the only time that the award was given to an entire nation. In 1993, Canada became the first country to issue gender guidelines for use in refugee determination. Moreover, in 2002, the Immigration and Refugee Protection Act took the important step of shifting the selection of resettlement refugees from the "ability to establish" to the need for protection, henceforth prioritizing humanitarian over economic considerations in refugee selection. Finally, whilst resettlement numbers fell from the early 2000s until the mid-2010s, the Trudeau government's decision to raise resettlement targets to bring in over 30,000 Syrian refugees in 2016 marked an important policy correction.

One striking exception within this laudatory assessment of Canada's resettlement policy is the Immigration Loan Program. The program requires resettled refugees to pay back – with interest, after a grace period – the costs of medical exams, travel documents, and transportation to Canada. It has been shown that the program compromises the ability of many refugees to pay for basic necessities and fully access settlement services – including language training – because of the need to earn income to commence loan repayment.[12] The program is petty, counterproductive, and at odds with Canada's humanitarian commitments. The government's decision to temporarily waive the repayment requirement for 25,000 of the Syrian refugees in 2016 was a step in the right direction, albeit one that did not go far enough. There is absolutely no reason why Canada should not "go all the way" and permanently scrap the Immigration Loan Program.

Whereas Canada's refugee resettlement policy has lived up to the 1976 Act's humanitarian commitments, the same cannot be said of its treatment of "spontaneous arrivals" – asylum applicants who file their claims in Canada. In striking contrast to Canada's humanitarian embrace of refugees selected from abroad, policymakers have been reluctant to welcome those seeking refuge at the border, even though both groups fall under the Refugee Convention. Since the turn of this century, a multitude of policy changes – ranging from mandatory detention of "designated" groups of asylum claimants to the Canadian-U.S. Safe Third Country Agreement, which allows Canada to turn back asylum applicants arriving its land border posts – have aggressively rolled back protections for the comparatively small number of those seeking asylum from within Canada. Over the past twenty years or so, policymakers have repeatedly driven a moral wedge between "deserving" resettled refugees and "undeserving" asylum claimants. After a boat with Sri Lankan asylum seekers arrived in British Columbia, Citizenship and Immigration Minister Jason Kenney warned that the arrival could put Canada at risk of developing "a two-tier immigration system – one tier for legal, law-abiding immigrants who patiently wait to come to the country, and a second tier who seek to come through the back door, typically through the asylum system."[13]

The portrayal of asylum claimants as queue-jumpers is devoid of any factual basis. Not only is there no such thing as an admission queue for refugees – there is no resettlement application that refugees could fill out – the Refugee Convention explicitly affirms the right of persons to seek asylum from persecution in other countries.[14] If we are to be serious about our commitment to refugee protection, then we will accept that it is our legal and moral duty to welcome those who claim asylum at our borders and offer them the opportunity of a hearing.

What is the verdict on the past fifty years of Canadian immigration policy? There are good reasons for why Canadian immigration policy – in particular our refugee resettlement policy and the point system – is commonly held up as a model to be emulated by policymakers abroad. In many ways, we have done an excellent job at "immigration management." We have been most true to our goals when admitting immigrants whose numbers we can easily manage from afar – such as resettlement refugees – or whose presence we consider to be in our economic interest – such as highly skilled immigrants. However, our reliance on immigration management and economically-driven immigration has come at a cost. When confronted with migration flows that cannot be easily managed or do not have predictable economic payoffs – as is the case with asylum claimants and elderly family members – our moral commitments have been too quickly abandoned. Managing immigration and recruiting immigrants for the sake of economic growth are legitimate policy goals. However, they must not displace Canada's commitment to family reunification and refugee protection.

NOTES

1 The author acknowledges the generous financial support of the Social Sciences and Humanities Research Council (Insight Grant #435-2013-1065).

I thank Graeme Bant for excellent research support and Alberto Alcaraz for copy-editing assistance.

2 Canada: Immigration Act, 1976–77, c. 52, s. 1

3 Department of Manpower and Immigration Canada, *Immigration Program: Green Paper on Immigration*, vol. 2 (Ottawa: Information Canada, 1974), 52, emphasis added.

4 Legislative Review Advisory Group, *A Canadian Framework for Future Immigration* (Ottawa: Minister of Public Works and Government Services Canada, 1997), 42.

5 The Immigration and Refugee Protection Act's extension of sponsorship rights to same-sex partners institutionalized and rendered transparent prior ad hoc and discretionary administrative practices.

6 As a third change, in recognition of the oftentimes delayed onset of independence, the sponsorship age for dependent children was raised from 19 to 22. The raising of the age ceiling for dependent children was subsequently reversed several times, most recently in 2014. It was reinstated in 2017.

7 It is worth noting that Canada's inclusive policy toward the reunification of immediate families stands in marked contrast to policies of civic integration currently in place in several European countries which have imposed high hurdles for the immigration of non-EU foreign spouses and have resulted in the lengthy separation of many families.

8 CBC News, "Don't Bring Parents Here for Welfare, Kenney Says," May 10, 2013.

9 Parliament of Canada, "Debate over New Immigration Regulations," *House of Commons Debates* 2 (February 27, 1962): 9.

10 Most notably, the Live-in Caregiver Program.

11 According to the United Nations' *Convention Relating to the Status of Refugees*.

12 Citizenship and Immigration Canada, "Evaluation of the Immigration Loan Program" (Ottawa: Citizenship and Immigration Canada, 2015).

13 Shauna Labman, "At Law's Border: Unsettling Refugee Resettlement" (PhD dissertation, University of British Columbia, 2012), 104.

14 Moreover, only 1 per cent of those identified by the United Nations High Commissioner for Refugees as in need of resettlement are actually selected for resettlement – globally speaking.

18 From Gérin-Lajoie to USMCA: The Role of the Canadian Provinces in Trade Negotiation

STÉPHANE PAQUIN

In *The Strategy of Conflict*, Nobel laureate Thomas Schelling developed a notion that is now known as "Schelling's conjecture." According to this conjecture, the United States executive is advantaged in its negotiation of a commercial treaty with another government when it is obvious that the legislature (Congress), which must ratify the treaty, has a firm stance on certain issues.

In a renegotiation such as the North American Free Trade Agreement (NAFTA), in which Congress will have a much larger role than in the past due to recent legislative changes, U.S. negotiators can therefore use this situation as a pretext for extracting additional concessions from their trading partners, Canada and Mexico.

Canada, where the separation of powers is more theoretical than real, cannot benefit from such a conjecture unless it has a minority government. In a majority context, the "threat" of seeing a defection of deputies of the party in power is rather weak and would not be credible.

In Canada other important actors in trade negotiations, the Canadian provinces, could have played the role of the U.S. Congress. But Ottawa decided not to involve them in the NAFTA/USMCA renegotiation. Federal refusal to involve the Canadian provinces has been a problem for a long time in Canada, and will become further fraught in the next fifty years since international treaties increasingly affect the fields of jurisdiction of the Canadian provinces.

In this article, I explain why provinces have become increasingly important players in Canada's international and trade negotiations. I begin by examining the evolution of treaty-making in Canada in general, which goes beyond trade issues. I then focus on trade negotiation with an emphasis on the NAFTA/USMCA renegotiations. I emphasize the case of Quebec since it has enhanced powers, compared to other provinces, when it comes to international agreements including trade agreements.

Federalism and International Negotiations in Canada

The 1867 Constitution Act gives little mention to international relations. In fact, Canada's constitution does not provide for exclusive jurisdiction over foreign affairs. This omission should not be surprising, for in 1867 Canada did not become sovereign; it became a dominion within the British Empire. Only with the passage of the 1931 Statute of Westminster did Canada become sovereign in matters of foreign policy. The question then quickly arose: does the federal government have the capacity to force the provinces to implement its treaties even in areas that, constitutionally, are under exclusive provincial jurisdiction?

In the Labour Conventions Case, the government of Ontario challenged the capacity of the Canadian government to legislate in provincial jurisdictions in order to fulfil its international commitments. After the 1930 election, Canada's Prime Minister, R.B. Bennett, ratified three International Labour Organization conventions: one on working hours, a second on weekly rest, and a third on the minimum wage. By imposing these conventions on the provinces, the Canadian government infringed on an area of provincial jurisdiction, labour.

The Judicial Committee of the Privy Council in London, which was still Canada's court of final appeal, rendered its judgment in 1937. This ruling is of fundamental importance for the legal capacity of the federal government and the rights of the provinces in international relations. The judges recalled that federalism constitutes the foundation of Canada. Furthermore, the principle of the sovereignty of Parliament means that the legislature is not obliged to pass measures that might be necessary to implement a treaty concluded by the federal executive. In this case then, it is up to the provincial legislatures (not the federal) to amend their respective laws and regulations to give effect to the treaty in domestic law. In Canada, the power to implement treaties thus follows the distribution of powers.

In addition to this situation, in 1965 Jean Lesage's Quebec government expressed its concern, as had Ontario before, over the effects of internationalization on provincial jurisdictions. In a speech in 1965, Quebec Vice Premier and Minister of Education Paul Gérin-Lajoie enunciated what would later become known as the "Gérin-Lajoie Doctrine of the international extension of Quebec's domestic jurisdictions," or "Gérin-Lajoie Doctrine" for short.[1] This doctrine basically holds that, when it is in its field of jurisdiction, Quebec should be the one negotiating the treaty. Moreover, since its enunciation, the government of Quebec has wanted to be involved in the Canadian delegation during international negotiation that affects its fields of jurisdiction.[2]

Furthermore, in 2002 Quebec's National Assembly unanimously passed an amendment to the Act Respecting the Ministère des Relations internationales, which requires National Assembly approval for any important international agreement entered into by Canada that concerns Quebec's fields of jurisdiction. The National Assembly has thus become the first parliament of the British model to be so closely involved in the process by which a central government undertakes international commitments. Daniel Turp has identified twenty-seven treaties concluded since 2002 by the federal government that were considered "important" and were therefore tabled for approval by the National Assembly of Quebec.[3] Thus, Quebec goes further than the federal government or any provinces, since the federal Parliament does not have to "approve" a treaty, although it must, as in Quebec, adopt legislation to assure its implementation.

In summary, since 1937 treaty-making in Canada has been a two-stage process comprised by: 1) conclusion of a treaty, that is, negotiation, signature and ratification; and 2) implementation. The first stage is the prerogative of the federal executive (a monopoly which has nonetheless been contested by the government of Quebec since the 1965 Gérin-Lajoie doctrine). The second stage, the passage of the necessary legislation to apply the treaty, is the prerogative of the legislative branch, federal and provincial. Treaties must thus be incorporated into domestic law by legislative action at the appropriate level. Judges base their rulings on Canadian laws, not treaties. The issue is of fundamental significance in Canada; as de Mestral and Fox-Decent point out, "roughly 40 per cent of federal statutes implement international rules in whole or in part."[4]

Trade Negotiations

In Canada, trade negotiations are in theory typically led by the federal government. This is in fact generally so, even when negotiations deal with an exclusive provincial jurisdiction. There are many precedents, though, in which provincial governments has been involved. Intergovernmental negotiations between senior bureaucrats and sometimes even ministers almost always take place.

The government of Canada here faces significant problems, for provincial collaboration is unavoidable when negotiations deal with the provinces' fields of jurisdiction. In Canada, there is no framework agreement providing for federal-provincial consultations, and there is very little consistency in the approach taken.[5] In addition, and even more significantly in the case of trade accords, the effects of treaties on domestic policy do not end with their implementation because they usually include dispute-settlement clauses.

For instance, since NAFTA does not apply directly in Canada, legislators amended Canadian law to conform to the treaty. Difficulties may emerge with respect to the dispute-settlement mechanism since judgments may require the offending state to amend its legislation or even revoke a past administrative decision. The question that then arises is whether the federal and provincial governments that implemented NAFTA committed themselves only with regard to the treaty or to future rulings by special groups as well.[6] The issue of the democratic deficit is thus cast into very sharp relief and may cause many problems, both legal and political.

The Canadian government contends that ratification of international treaties is the sole prerogative of the federal executive. It may commit Canada internationally with no form of consent from federal or provincial legislatures, even if a treaty should require substantial changes to laws and regulations. To avoid foreseeable problems, some authors, like de Mestral and Fox-Decent argue the federal government does not ratify international treaties that necessitate legislative changes by the provinces without prior provincial approval.[7]

I disagree with this affirmation. In fact, though, a detailed examination of the legislative steps involved in concluding a treaty reveals a relatively long process that is often not completed before ratification by Canada.[8] Take, for example, the two NAFTA side agreements on the environment and labour, which in Canada are exclusive (labour) or shared (environment) provincial fields of jurisdiction. Most of the provinces wished to take part in the negotiations on them, but the federal government wanted to act alone. The negotiations resulted in a clause that would permit provinces to withdraw from the side agreements.[9] Only three provinces have since signed the environment agreement (Alberta in 1995, Quebec in 1996, and Manitoba in 1997) and only four have signed the labour agreement (Alberta in 1995, Quebec and Manitoba in 1996, and Prince Edward Island in 1998).[10]

The NAFTA side-agreements are not exceptional in this regard. Canada signed a Free Trade Agreement with Costa Rica on 23 April 2001. The implementation legislation was tabled on 20 September 2001; royal assent was given on 18 December 2001; and the treaty entered into force on 1 November 2002.[11] Quebec's National Assembly approved the treaty only on 2 June 2004.

Similarly, the Government of Canada signed the Canada-Chile Free Trade Agreement on 5 December 1996. The House of Commons passed the implementation legislation on 5 July1997. The treaty was not approved by the government of Quebec until 3 June 2004, seven years after it had come into effect.[12]

Trade Negotiations and the Canadian Provinces

In Canada, provinces have thus become increasingly important players in international trade. In the case of Quebec, approximately 40 per cent of the 750 international agreements concluded by the government (of which 386 are currently in force) have a direct or indirect link to trade, relating to areas such as economic development, agriculture, culture, natural resources, and public procurement.[13] Significant agreements include the 2001 Intergovernmental Agreement on Government Procurement with the State of New York, the 2008 Quebec-France Agreement on the Mutual Recognition of Professional Qualifications, and the 2013 Agreement on the Creation of a Carbon Market with the State of California. These three agreements all have a direct impact on trade.

NAFTA/USMCA Renegotiations

In the case of the renegotiation of NAFTA, the Government of Canada chose to exclude the provinces from renegotiation despite a request from the Quebec government. The provinces are essentially informed of the unfolding and the stakes of the negotiation by a federal-provincial mechanism called the C-trade meetings, a forum that essentially brings together federal and provincial civil servants who manage trade issues. A high-level representative from the Ontario government described the forum as an "information dump," a forum where federal public servants, with little notice, release a large volume of documents for analysis. This approach has the effect that provincial feedback is minimal in the NAFTA renegotiation process.[14]

It can be hypothesized that the federal government wanted to do this because the U.S. government was pushing for quick renegotiation and that giving the provinces a place in the Canadian delegation would slow down the pace of negotiation. Yet, during the renegotiation, time was exactly what the Government of Canada needed. Canada's best bet in the renegotiation was to buy time so that U.S. Congress, civil society, and the American business community have the time to organize to oppose the president.

The Canadian government also developed a renegotiation strategy, an "idealist agenda," that put issues on the table in its list of positive requests. Canada did not want to be in a purely defensive position during the renegotiation, because the inevitable concessions in a negotiation would force them to make difficult choices.

As a result, Canada has developed "demands," many of which are under the jurisdiction of, or have very significant effects on, provincial legislation. The Government of Canada wants to strengthen the chapter on labour and labour mobility (labour protection, unions rights), the environment and climate change, gender, First Nations, arbitration mechanisms, and public procurement of provinces and municipal governments. These are very important and deep intrusions into provincial jurisdictions. On the negative list (what Canada does not want to see in the treaty), many subjects are also very important for the provinces, such as softwood lumber, cultural exception or diversity clause, supply management, and Chapter 19, on dispute settlement.

But there is more: many U.S. demands in the renegotiation affect directly provincial measures such as rules of origins, market access for milk, grain, wine, and cars, the cultural exception, supply management in agriculture, softwood lumber, e-commerce and provincial, municipal, and territorial government procurement, and Chapter 19.

Conclusion

The federal government has always had some important reservations in involving the provinces in international negotiations. In the case of the NAFTA/USMCA renegotiation, provinces might have to pay the price of the federal strategy. The biggest argument against provincial involvement is related to the fact that it will slow down the process and make it hard to make concessions. That might be true in some cases, but keep in mind that Canada successfully concluded a very ambitious and deep international trade agreement with the European Union with an unprecedented representations of the Canadian provinces. Indeed, for the first time in the history of Canadian trade negotiations, the provinces were represented in the Canadian delegation, and even participated directly in negotiations on several subjects.[15]

The important role of the provinces, and of Quebec in particular, has been recognized and encouraged by Justin Trudeau's federal government. The Quebec premier, Phillipe Couillard, was even invited to travel to Belgium, with Jean Charest and Pierre Marc Johnson (former PM and Quebec chief negotiator), alongside the Canadian Prime Minister for the formal signing of the agreement.[16]

No doubt, it is time to rethink intergovernmental relations with regards to trade relations in Canada.

NOTES

1 Stéphane Paquin, "Le Fédéralisme et Les Relations Internationales Du Canada Depuis Le Jugement de 1937 Sur Les Conventions de Travail," in *Le Prolongement Externe Des Compétences Internes: Les Relations Internationales Du Québec Depuis La Doctrine Gérin-Lajoie (1965–2005)*, ed. Stéphane Paquin (Ste-Foy: Presses de l'Université Laval, 2006), 7–24.

2 Ministère des Relations internationales et de la Francophonie, "Le Québec dans le monde: s'investir, agir, prospérer," 2017, 30, https://www.mrif.gouv.qc.ca/content/documents/fr/PIQ_DocumentLong_FR-NUM.pdf.

3 Daniel Turp, "L'Approbation Des Engagements Internationaux Importants Du Quebec: La Nouvelle Dimension Parlementaire a La Doctrine Gerin-Lajoie," *Revue Québécoise de Droit International* Hors-série (Juin 2016): 9–40.

4 Armand de Mestral and Evan Fox-Decent, "Rethinking the Relationship between International and Domestic Law," *McGill Law Journal* 53, no. 4 (2008): 573–648.

5 Armand de Mestral, "The Provinces and International Relations in Canada," in *The States and Moods of Federalism: Governance, Identity and Methodology*, ed. J.-F. Gaudreau-DesBiens and F. Gélinas (Cowansville: Éditions Yvon Blais, 2005), 319–22.

6 Minister of Justice, Members of panels (NAFTA) regulations SOR/94-117, May 2018, http://laws.justice.gc.ca/PDF/SOR-94-117.pdf.

7 de Mestral and Fox-Decent, "Rethinking the Relationship between International and Domestic Law."

 8 Stéphane Paquin, "Federalism and Compliance with International Agree-
    ments: Belgium and Canada Compared," *The Hague Journal of Diplomacy* 5,
    no. 1–2 (January 2010): 173–97.
 9 Chris Kukucha, "Domestic Politics and Canadian Foreign Trade Policy:
    Intrusive Interdependence, the WTO and the NAFTA," *Canadian Foreign
    Policy Journal* 10, no. 2 (January 1, 2003): 59–85.
10 Stéphane Paquin, "Federalism and the Governance of International Trade
    Negotiations in Canada: Comparing CUSFTA with CETA," *International
    Journal* 68, no. 4 (December 1, 2013): 548.
11 Paquin, "Federalism and Compliance with International Agreements,"
    192–3.
12 Paquin, 193.
13 Richard Ouellet and Guillaume Beaumier, "L'activité du Québec en
    matière de commerce international: de l'énonciation de la doctrine Gérin-
    Lajoie à la négociation de l'AECG," *Revue Québécoise de Droit International*,
    Hors-série (Juin 2016): 67–79.
14 Stéphane Paquin, "Le Rôle Des Provinces Dans La Renégociation de
    l'ALENA," *Policy Options*, July 25, 2017, 173–97.
15 Paquin, "Federalism and the Governance of International Trade
    Negotiations in Canada"; Christopher J. Kukucha, "Provincial/Territorial
    Governments and the Negotiation of International Trade Agreements,"
    IRPP Insight, no. 10 (October 2016): 16; J. Anthony VanDuzer, "Could
    an Intergovernmental Agreement Increase the Credibility of Canadian
    Treaty Commitments in Areas within Provincial Jurisdiction?," *Interna-
    tional Journal* 68, no. 4 (December 1, 2013): 536–44; Patrick Fafard and
    Patrick Leblond, "Closing the Deal: What Role for the Provinces in the
    Final Stages of the CETA Negotiations?," *International Journal* 68, no.
    4 (December 1, 2013): 553–9.
16 Raphaël Bouvier-Auclair, "L'accord de libre-échange Canada-UE est
    signé," *Radio Canada*, October 30, 2016, http://ici.radio-canada.ca/
    nouvelle/811713/canada-ue-libre-echange.

19 Canada and the World: Managing Insecurity in a Changing Global Order

Once upon a time, Canada was a champion of global peacekeeping.[1] That time was over fifty years ago. During this "golden age," Canada made significant troop contributions to United Nations (UN) missions around the world, and enthusiastically advocated for the newly minted international institutions of the post-1945 global order.[2] This liberal internationalist approach to foreign policy bolstered Canada's influence, allowing it to punch above its mid-sized weight class.[3]

The end of the Cold War in 1991, however, sparked a new wave of complex civil wars, making peacekeeping far more perilous. The frustrating crisis in Bosnia, brutal genocide in Rwanda, and horrifying atrocities in Somalia during the mid-1990s dampened Canadian enthusiasm for international missions in highly-fragmented and volatile states. Over the next two decades, Canadian peacekeeping commitments systematically declined, reaching all-time lows.[4]

In 2015, Liberal Prime Minister Justin Trudeau announced a revival of the Canadian peacekeeping tradition. Yet, after multiple delays, the long-awaited November 2017 announcement included no new troop commitments to any United Nations mission. What explains these changes in Canadian security policy over the past fifty years? Looking ahead, how will Canada respond to the new security threats of the twenty-first century?

To answer these crucial questions, it is essential to contextualize decisions made on Parliament Hill within the wider international system. Indeed, when it comes to security policy, Canadian decisions – both in peacekeeping and warfighting – have always been shaped and constrained by great power politics. Canadian behaviour on the world stage not only reflects domestic values and interests, but also the global order, which is subject to both rapid shocks and gradual decay. As that order changes, so too does the global conflict landscape, and thus Canada's engagement of it. The future of Canadian security policy is therefore not entirely in the hands of Canadians.

To unpack these meta-level processes, in the following sections I focus on three distinct post–Second World War periods of global order: the bipolar world order during the height of the Cold War in the 1960s, the unipolar world order in the 1990s following the fall of the Soviet Union, and the new multipolar world order emerging as a result of American hegemonic decline. I propose that these three distinct world orders have had seismic effects on both global conflict processes and Canada's role in them. Future Canadian security policies will therefore necessarily be shaped by an emerging new world order and the choices our key allies will make within that global space.

Bipolarity

Fifty years ago, at the height of the Cold War, states were overwhelmingly concerned with their survival. The near-catastrophic 1962 Cuban missile crisis had revealed both the existential threat of nuclear annihilation and the unclear and dangerous diplomacy and communication between the White House and the Kremlin.[5] For Canadians, the crisis also revealed the challenges of maintaining an alliance with a nuclear superpower. Indeed, Prime Minister John G. Diefenbaker, who saw the Americans as too reckless during the crisis, strained already-tense relations with President John F. Kennedy by refusing to take a hardline position on Cuba. In the global standoff between East and West, Canada was both indebted to the United States for its security and desperate for independence from its grip.

It was through its peacekeeping mandate that Canada established its distinctive international voice. While the paralysed United Nations Security Council was unable to prevent conflict between the great powers, the UN remained a useful venue for international cooperation on other matters. Building on its success in peacekeeping during the 1956 Suez Crisis, Canada thus advocated that the UN play an important role in addressing a slew of smaller scale interstate conflicts of global relevance.[6]

Peacekeeping quickly became a Canadian brand, popular at home and abroad. The peacekeeping missions it joined typically involved monitoring and implementing armistices between states; this work was challenging and admirable, but not overwhelmingly perilous. Canada thereby established a global presence through its support of UN institutions, increasing its profile and soft power influence.

Of course, the reason that Canada had the freedom to champion this peacekeeping and liberal internationalist agenda during the Cold War was precisely because its core defensive security interests had been secured through its U.S. security alliances, including the North Atlantic Treaty Organization (NATO) and North American Aerospace Defence Command (NORAD). Geographic realities cemented the U.S.-Canada alliance, and nuclear deterrence became a continental affair.

By 1963, Prime Minister Lester B. Pearson allowed the United States to deploy nuclear-tipped missiles on Canadian soil as part of continental defence efforts.[7] By leaning on American superpower to meet its core defensive needs, Canada enjoyed the freedom to invest its military resources in peacekeeping. Embracing the peacekeeping mantle allowed Canada to forge an identity that distinguished it from its more powerful southern neighbour without compromising its core U.S. alliance.

While Canada was focused on peacekeeping, however, the great powers had initiated a new form of warfighting. In 1960, the UN General Assembly passed its historic Declaration on the Granting of Independence to Colonial Countries and Peoples. Colonized peoples around the world mobilized against European imperialism and demanded their sovereignty, resulting in wave of new liberation movements. Behind the scenes, however, both the Soviet Union and the United States were actively coopting these newly independent states.

Because nuclear deterrence prevented the great powers from engaging in direct confrontations, the Americans and Soviets fought their battles in these newly postcolonial states. In a bloody chess match for global influence, both superpowers pumped weapons and resources to movements and regimes across Africa, Latin America, and Asia. National anticolonial struggles quickly transformed into Cold-War proxy wars. Countries like Vietnam and Afghanistan became battlegrounds for American and Soviet power.

Canada remained on the sidelines of these conflicts, and Pearson even criticized the United States for the reckless and costly Vietnam War. Ironically, once the Cold War came to an end, Canada's commitment to peacekeeping brought it back into the very heart of these old proxy war battlefields.

Unipolarity

After nearly fifty years of intense rivalry, in 1991 the Soviet Union dissolved and the United States emerged as the world's only superpower. Relations thawed between East and West, and the UN Security Council was no longer paralysed. The Cold War ended without a direct confrontation between the great powers, and a new global order of American hegemony emerged.

For much of the world, however, this power transition was incredibly violent. Countries that had served as proxies of either the United States or the Soviet Union lost their great power sponsors. Many collapsed into brutal conflicts along ethnic, tribal, and sectarian lines. New civil wars around the world erupted in deadly and complex cycles of violence, fuelled by stockpiles of leftover American and Soviet-grade weaponry.[8]

In 1991, Somalia collapsed into brutal clan-based civil war. That same year, the former Yugoslavia erupted in ethnic and sectarian violence. By 1992, Afghanistan was awash in ethnic cleansing campaigns. Two years later, Rwanda was consumed by genocide. Cold War proxy wars had given way to ethnic conflict. As the atrocities mounted, the international community called for peacekeepers to quell the violence.

Given the complexity of these conflicts, the UN envisioned a new approach to intervention. In 1992, then-UN Secretary General Boutros Boutros-Ghali penned "An Agenda for Peace," which drastically redefined the parameters of peacekeeping missions.[9] This approach placed a much heavier emphasis on peace creation and peace enforcement in places where that were ensnared in violent conflict.

Upholding the peacekeeping mantle, Canada answered this call to action, and then quickly became embroiled in operations far more volatile than traditional peacekeeping. In the former Yugoslavia, Canadian peacekeepers were placed under warfighting conditions, while also shackled by UN regulations on the use of force. The result was disastrous.[10] Indeed, the UN declared Srebrenica a "safe zone" for Bosnian civilians, and then failed to provide sufficient peacekeepers to hold off the Bosnian Serb Army. The resulting massacre at Srebrenica became the worst case of ethnic cleansing in Europe since the Second World War.[11] It was only through a sustained NATO air bombing campaign in 1995 that the Serbs were finally forced to the negotiating table, ending the three-and-a-half-year conflict with the signing of the Dayton Accords.[12]

The challenges of modern peacekeeping were even more apparent in the disastrous 1992–95 UN peacekeeping mission to Somalia. The

Somalia mission was originally intended to secure the delivery of humanitarian aid during a famine. Yet as the tribal war escalated, predatory militias rapaciously looted the humanitarian aid. Frustrated, the peacekeepers tried to protect the aid from the looters, but in doing so, accidentally took sides against rival clans.[13] The crisis came to a head by 1993, most notably with the infamous downing of an American Black Hawk helicopter and grisly murder of U.S. troops on the streets of Mogadishu.

For Canadians, the Somalia mission was a disgrace. A national inquiry into the Somalia mission found that members of the Canadian Airborne Regiment (CAR) had baited, tortured, and murdered Somali children.[14] The scandal not only tarnished Canada's global reputation, but also shattered Canadian confidence in peacekeeping. After Canadian forces withdrew from Somalia, the CAR was completely disbanded, and in the years ahead, military budgets were slashed.

Following the disaster in Somalia, both the United States and Canada were wary of embarking on any new peacekeeping operations in complex war theatres, especially on the African continent. Thus, when the UN mission in Rwanda called for action on the 1994 genocide, the global response was muted. As the international community balked, genocide exploded; within 100 days, over 800,000 Tutsis were murdered by Hutu militias.[15] In the aftermath of the genocide, world leaders apologized for failing to "do more." Yet by the mid-1990s, peacekeeping commitments had dropped, both in Canada and around the world.

The era of unipolarity eased tensions between the great powers, but also birthed a new breed of civil war not easily contained through peacekeeping. The civil war literature clearly shows that in conflicts with many actors, each can act to spoil peace processes.[16] Scholarly research also shows that conflicts that are funded by deeply-entrenched war economies are both lengthy and brutally violent.[17] Peacekeeping under these conditions is bloody, costly, and high-risk; in the mid- to late-1990s, Canada held back.[18]

In 2001, however, Canadian security policy pivoted sharply. After the 9/11 attacks, the United States invoked Article 5 of the NATO Charter, calling on its allies to come to its defence. Responding to the American call for allied support, Canada deployed forces to Afghanistan from 2001 to 2014 under a NATO mandate to combat Taliban insurgents in the country. Canada assumed the heavy responsibility of fighting insurgents in the volatile southern province of Kandahar, in what became the longest military mission in its history.

This was warfighting, not peacekeeping. Yet, much like the complex peacekeeping missions of the early 1990s, the fact that Afghanistan suffered from high levels of ethnic fragmentation, a slew of spoiler groups, and a thriving war economy presented Canadian forces with a myriad of military, political, and ethical challenges. Canada's Afghan partners, both in office and in the trenches, were frustrating and problematic throughout the war. The post-Taliban government was comprised of a multitude of ethnic warlords and criminal bosses with astonishing records of corruption and abuse.[19] While Canadians were trying to stabilize Kandahar, the brother of former Afghan President Hamid Karzai was secretly running the province as a powerful drug lord. This corruption was pervasive. Indeed, the current Vice President General Abdul Rashid Dostum, an infamous Uzbek warlord, stands accused of personally raping the governor of Jowzjan Province, Ahmad Ishchi, in a feud.

With such problematic local partners, Canada once again became ensnared in controversy. Reminiscent of the Somalia Affair, in 2007 Canadian troops were accused of involvement in torture. As details of the scandal emerged, allegations were levied against Canadian soldiers who had detained suspected militants and had then handed them over to local Afghan security forces to be tortured. Under international law, Canada was responsible for the treatment of prisoners that it detained, and could therefore be liable for torture perpetrated by the Afghan security forces that NATO had partnered with. The allegations damaged Canadian confidence in the mission.[20]

After the last Canadian troops withdrew from Afghanistan in 2014, Canadians began a difficult national conversation about what the mission had accomplished. Whether or not Canada was "successful" remains the subject of much debate. What is clear, however, is why Canada went to Afghanistan in the first place. This was a call of duty, for the collective defence of the United States. It was the only instance in NATO history when a member state invoked the Article 5 collective security clause. For more than twelve years, Canadians fought and died to honour these NATO obligations, and defend their American allies.

Multipolarity

History shows that the rise and fall of great powers is part of the long-term, natural evolution of the international system. Over the past decade, scholars of international relations have tracked the rise of China, the resurgence of Russia, the emergence of regional great powers, and the decline of American global power.[21] Some experts have held onto the idea that American hegemony could endure indefinitely; since 2016, however, most of these scholars have accepted the reality that the global order is changing.[22] The era of American unipolarity is coming to an end. A new multipolar world order is on the horizon.

The historical record shows that these types of large-scale great power transitions are inherently dangerous. In the past century alone, there have been three major shifts in the global balance of power, each incredibly violent. The First World War cost 25 million lives in four years. The Second World War resulted in 60 million deaths in six years. The end of the Cold War, while peaceful between the great powers, sparked brutal civil wars across the globe. It would be folly to assume the current great power transition will involve no risk. Indeed, power transition theorists contend that a shift from unipolarity to multipolarity can trigger major war.[23] The 2016 election of mercurial U.S. President Donald Trump further increases unpredictability during this volatile period.

Amid these global changes, the U.S.-Canadian relationship is also fragile. A decline in American global power will have a serious effect on Canada, which is inextricably bound to the United States by shared geography, economic ties, and alliance commitments. Yet, never before has a sitting American president threatened to abandon the security alliances that have defended the Western Hemisphere since the end of the Second World War. Never before has an incoming American president called the leader of a rival state before reaching out to the Canadian Prime Minister. President Trump's unusual relationship with Moscow, his declarations that NATO is either "obsolete" or "no longer obsolete," and his demands that NATO members "pay up," have undermined confidence in the alliance and heightened fears of both misperception and miscalculation along the Russian border – and just as Canadian troops were deployed to Latvia under a NATO mandate. In the Middle East, the United States has also reversed its position, declaring in May 2018 that it would withdraw its commitment to the 2015 deal that curtailed the Iranian nuclear program. Meanwhile in the Pacific, American sabre-rattling and mixed-signalling has escalated tensions with North Korea, a regime that has demonstrated its increased nuclear capabilities, and which threatens to shift polarities in a region where China has historically held regional hegemonic power. This American unpredictability has intensified security dilemmas across the globe.

Given this ongoing uncertainty, it is therefore no surprise that Canada has scaled back its peacekeeping revival. In November 2017, Canada declared that it would not make any significant commitments of peace-keepers, and would rather assist existing missions and contribute niche resources to future peacekeeping efforts. To that end, in March 2018 Canada agreed to send a modest contribution of six military helicopters and 250 troops to Mali in order to support medical evacuations and UN transport operations in the war-torn northern region. The announcement disappointed UN members who hoped for a 600-troop boost in Mali, a conflict zone marked by a highly-fragmented state, multiple ethnic factions, and a criminalized war economy.

For Ottawa, however, the primary security concerns facing Canada in the months and years ahead lie in neither the deserts of Mali nor the mountains of Afghanistan; they are immediately south of the border. During this fraught period of global power transition, the most critical security challenge facing Canada will be the maintenance of the alliance with the United States, and the peaceful management of the transition to a new multipolar world order. Unpredictability and volatility during great power transitions provokes major war. In the months and years ahead, Canada must use its diplomatic leverage and soft power influence to mitigate disaster between the great powers. And when necessary, lay low and ride out the storm.

NOTES

1 The author thanks the Norwegian Research Council for its support of this research.
2 Adam Chapnick, "'A Great Small Country on the International Scene': Looking Back at Canada and the United Nations," *International Journal* 67, no. 4 (2012): 1063–72.
3 Erika Simpson, "The Principles of Liberal Internationalism According to Lester Pearson," *Journal of Canadian Studies* 34, no. 1 (February 1, 1999): 75–92.
4 Roland Paris, "Are Canadians Still Liberal Internationalists? Foreign Policy and Public Opinion in the Harper Era," *International Journal: Canada's Journal of Global Policy Analysis* 69, no. 3 (September 1, 2014): 274–307.
5 Don Munton and David A. Welch, *The Cuban Missile Crisis: A Concise History* (New York: Oxford University Press, 2011).
6 Robert C. Thomsen and Nikola Hynek, "Keeping the Peace and National Unity: Canada's National and International Identity Nexus," *International Journal* 61, no. 4 (December 1, 2006): 845–58.

7   John Clearwater, *Canadian Nuclear Weapons: The Untold Story of Canada's Cold War Arsenal* (Dundurn, 1998).
8   Stathis N. Kalyvas, "'New' and 'Old' Civil Wars: A Valid Distinction?," *World Politics* 54, no. 1 (2001): 99–118.
9   Aisha Ahmad, "Agenda for Peace or Budget for War: Evaluating the Economic Impact of International Intervention in Somalia," *International Journal* 67 (2012 2011): 313.
10 Peter Andreas, *Blue Helmets and Black Markets: The Business of Survival in the Siege of Sarajevo* (Cornell University Press, 2011).
11 David Rohde, *Endgame: The Betrayal and Fall of Srebrenica, Europe's Worst Massacre Since World War II* (Penguin, 2012).
12 Andrew L. Stigler, "A Clear Victory for Air Power: NATO's Empty Threat to Invade Kosovo," *International Security* 27, no. 3 (January 1, 2003): 124–57.
13 Ahmad, "Agenda for Peace or Budget for War."
14 Sherene Razack, *Dark Threats and White Knights: The Somalia Affair, Peacekeeping, and the New Imperialism* (Toronto: University of Toronto Press, 2004); Grant Dawson, *"Here Is Hell": Canada's Engagement in Somalia* (Vancouver: UBC Press, 2011).
15 Romeo Dallaire, *Shake Hands with the Devil: The Failure of Humanity in Rwanda* (New York: Carroll & Graf, 2004).
16 Stephen John Stedman, "Spoiler Problems in Peace Processes," *International Security* 22, no. 2 (October 1, 1997): 5–53; David E. Cunningham, "Veto Players and Civil War Duration," *American Journal of Political Science* 50, no. 4 (October 2006): 875–92; Kristin M. Bakke, Kathleen Gallagher Cunningham, and Lee J.M. Seymour, "A Plague of Initials: Fragmentation, Cohesion, and Infighting in Civil Wars," *Perspectives on Politics* 10, no. 2 (June 2012): 265–83.
17 William Reno, *Warlord Politics and African States* (Boulder, Colo.: Lynne Rienner Publishers, 1998); Paul Collier and Anke Hoefller, "Greed and Grievance in Civil War," *Oxford Economic Papers* 56, no. 4 (2004): 563–95; Jeremy M. Weinstein, *Inside Rebellion: The Politics of Insurgent Violence* (Cambridge: Cambridge University Press, 2007); Aisha Ahmad, "The Security Bazaar: Business Interests and Islamist Power in Civil War Somalia," *International Security* 39, no. 3 (January 1, 2015): 89–117.
18 Pierre Martin and Michel Fortmann, "Canadian Public Opinion and Peacekeeping in a Turbulent World: Peacekeeping's New Look," *International Journal* 50 (1995): 370–400.
19 Dipali Mukhopadhyay, *Warlords, Strongman Governors, and the State in Afghanistan* (Cambridge: Cambridge University Press, 2014).

20 In 2011, Canada also participated in a seven-month UN-authorized NATO mission in Libya, under the Responsibility to Protect (R2P) doctrine. This disastrous intervention collapsed the Libyan state, created an all-new civil war, and birthed an extremist insurgency and war economy. For a discussion on the R2P doctrine, see Gareth Evans, Ramesh Thakur, and Robert A. Pape, "Correspondence: Humanitarian Intervention and the Responsibility to Protect," *International Security* 37, no. 4 (2013): 199–214.

21 Michael Beckley, "China's Century? Why America's Edge Will Endure," *International Security* 36, no. 3 (December 28, 2011): 41–78; Arvind Subramanian, "The Inevitable Superpower," *Foreign Affairs*, August 19, 2011, https://www.foreignaffairs.com/articles/china/2011-08-19/inevitable-superpower; Joshua R. Itzkowitz Shifrinson and Michael Beckley, "Debating China's Rise and U.S. Decline," *International Security* 37, no. 3 (December 13, 2012): 172–81; Stephen G. Brooks and William C. Wohlforth, "The Rise and Fall of the Great Powers in the Twenty-First Century: China's Rise and the Fate of America's Global Position," *International Security* 40, no. 3 (January 1, 2016): 7–53.

22 Carla Norrlof, *America's Global Advantage: US Hegemony and International Cooperation* (Cambridge: Cambridge University Press, 2010); Carla Norrlof, "America-First Ideology Will Trigger American Decline," *The Globe and Mail*, November 14, 2018, https://www.theglobeandmail.com/opinion/america-first-ideology-will-trigger-american-decline/article32837024/.

23 A.F.K. Organski, *World Politics* (New York: Random House, 1968).

20 Has Canada Reached Policy Gridlock?

PETER JOHN LOEWEN AND ANDREW POTTER

What is the future of policymaking in Canada? It is tempting to suggest, as the saying goes, that the future will resemble the past, but even more so. That is, we might suppose that the policy challenges of the next fifty years will be more or less the same as the ones of the last half-century, but weighed down by the accretions of decades of wrangling.

A glance at the table of contents of this volume reinforces that view. The core topics – including immigration and multiculturalism, federal-provincial relationships, and aboriginal governance – have been the meat and potatoes of Canadian governance for decades now, and the analyses offered here give every indication that the policy fights in these arenas are far from settled.

But if you scan the headlines or your social media feed, you will get a much different sense of the agenda. Dealing with the products of Silicon Valley alone will be enough to occupy policymakers for a generation – from the platforms (Facebook, Google, Uber, Amazon) to CRISPr to drones to the privatization and commercialization of space to autonomous cars – and every week seems to bring a new technology or new development that threatens to overturn the foundations of the social and economic order.

But even if we set aside the incessant and more or less unpredictable technological evolution that colours every assumption about what the future will be like, the policy landscape of the next fifty years is looking, if not radically changed, at least tilted in a different direction from what we have faced in the past. It is starting to look as though the assumptions that have guided policymaking in the past, and the solutions we have developed to our biggest challenges, will be more hindrance than help in the future.

To illustrate this, we can look at four main areas in which Canada has devoted its policy energies over the last few decades. These include Canada-U.S. relations, the balance between the federal government and the provinces and territories, immigration, and resource development. In all four areas, major policy successes have, rather than serving as a model for future problem solving, only generated a new set of even more intractable problems.

1. The history of Canada is marked by a love-hate relationship with the United States, which has been characterized by two contending dynamics. On the one hand, the fear of domination by our neighbour to the south has fuelled successive nationalist movements, of which Confederation itself is the most notable example. But this has been countered by an equal and opposite fear of being cut off from the American market. And so, even as Canadians have fought for political and cultural independence from the United States, they have sued for economic reciprocity. The culmination of this, the Free Trade Agreement of 1989 and its continental successor, NAFTA, secured our access to the continental market. But it also locked Canada into a complacency trap, to the point where fully 75 per cent of all "exports" are to the United States. This has made us hugely dependent on the United States and – as we are rediscovering in the age of Donald Trump and new protectionism – hugely vulnerable to the periodic waves of American isolationism.

The North American Free Trade Agreement has provided both benefits and challenges. Through a sustained and structured trade relationship, we have experienced the benefits of rules-based, predictable trade. Indeed, through dozens of other trade agreements enacted or in process since NAFTA, governments of both Conservative and Liberal stripes have demonstrated an ability to export these rules-based arrangements and to expand commerce for Canadian firms, while reducing the price of goods and services for Canadians. A large part of this success is underwritten by our ability to present ourselves as an effective point of entry for an American market. These are all the upsides to first learning to trade with the United States and then exporting this model to other arrangements.

The downside is that NAFTA has worked so well – on purely economic measures, rather than on political criteria – that we have had little experience with renegotiation or conflict resolution. When we have been confronted with such conflicts, as in the challenges presented by President Trump, our response has often been to make appeals based on shared values and interests, rather than on the simple rules of the game. Often, we seek exceptions that are not available to other partners based on this comity. While this may work in the short term, it suggests to our other long term partners that we have not fully learned the lessons of rules-based trade. We are instead still willing to play to regional and cultural familiarity. This is ultimately an obstacle, and perhaps a major one, to diversifying trade and more fully integrating economically with Europe, Asia, and South America.

2. With respect to federal-provincial relations, Canadians are familiar with the standard story, which is that the country was designed to have a strong central government with the provinces eventually degenerating into mere municipalities (as Sir John A. Macdonald famously envisioned). But thanks to various structural features of the federation and a number of crucial rulings by the Judicial Committee of the Privy Council, the balance steadily shifted, with the provinces developing into mini-states held together in an increasingly confederal set of arrangements.

We've given this structure a number of names over the years, calling it "executive federalism" or "cooperative federalism" or "open federalism," but it all basically means the same thing, namely, the provinces individually or severally extract power, money, or other political concessions out of Ottawa in exchange for relatively little. The result is a federal government that transfers a lot of money around the country, and plays a useful convening role in trying to focus attention on questions of national importance, but is actually unable or even afraid to wield direct power even in areas in which it has clear jurisdiction.

A lot has been achieved under this rubric, including the creation of the universal provision of health care, a thriving postsecondary sector, and impressive industrial development. But the downside is that we might have reached the point where the federal government is no longer able to exercise one of its key functions, which is to resolve collective action problems amongst the provinces and prevent the flourishing of beggar-thy-neighbour activities. Consider just two examples. First, there remain severe restrictions on the movement of both goods and labour across provincial boundaries. This is underwritten by protectionist professional associations and provinces jealous of excise revenues, among other things. But it is also aided by a federal government that has so balkanized the availability of government services, through substantial cross-country variation in employment insurance, and an ineffective and invidious equalization program, that it too has little genuine interest in substantial mobility amongst the citizenry. The movement of goods and services has further been hampered by a Supreme Court that largely fails to understand the value of commercial competition across provincial boundaries. Second, the federal government appears unable to facilitate the construction of national energy infrastructure, short of effective nationalization. We say more on this below.

The upshot is that instead of an active federal government creating and enforcing national markets and a meaningful national citizenship, what Canadian federalism has increasingly been about is allowing ever-stronger provinces to flex their muscles in the face of an increasingly weak and ineffectual central government. This may have been a forced decision, given the existential threat of Quebec sovereignty and the real possibility of other secessionist movements emerging, but it has also not obviously made us wealthier or better governed. Most importantly, it has made concrete a mindset in which the federal government is not assumed to be able to take the domestic actions in the national interest that most other national governments take for granted.

3. If there has been one great Canadian policy success story in the last fifty years, it is our approach to immigration and multiculturalism. For all the 1980s stereotyping over Canada being a "mosaic" and the handwringing in the 1990s over so-called "hyphenated Canadians," the truth is a lot more straightforward. As Will Kymlicka has taught us, multiculturalism is best understood not as an *identity*, but as a *policy* designed to offer immigrants fair and reasonable terms of integration into national institutions.

And in that, there can be no doubt that we have been enormously successful. We have brought in over 200,000 immigrants a year – more than 300,000 in recent years – for close to three decades. We now have the second-highest proportion of foreign born residents in the world, behind Australia. Despite this, support for immigration remains high, notwithstanding the waves of anti-immigrant sentiment that have swept over parts of Europe and the United States in recent years. We would wager that Canada can continue to largely resist this sentiment and continue a policy of well-managed immigration for decades to come, through a combination of luck (our border consists of three oceans and the United States of America) and good policymaking (we offer a relatively easy path to naturalization, and we have an immigration policy that brings in people from all over the world, as a result of which no one group dominates within the migrant population).

But there are still two policy problems at the core of this, neither of which can be ignored.

First, there is increasing evidence that new Canadians do not enjoy economic and social integration at the rate that previous generations of immigrants did. Canadians of longer standing – whether so called "old stock" Canadians or those who immigrated in more recent generations – may view new immigrants as a drain on social services and a strain on the social fabric. Perceptions matter here as much as realities. The reaction to this is often a call for less immigration and social and economic isolation of those exact people thought to be stressing the system. These two related pressures can provide massive challenges for immigration policy, and related policies around social and economic integration.

Second, the last few years have seen a growing recognition that even as we have successfully integrated millions of newcomers into our national fabric, our Indigenous peoples remain strikingly marginalized. And indeed, from the Indigenous perspective the two phenomena are related: by bringing in successive waves of newcomers, Canadians have simply recruited millions of immigrants into their original settler ambitions. And thus we have arrived at the uncomfortable position where one of our greatest policy success stories, immigration, is in direct tension with one of our greatest failures, Indigenous reconciliation. This is not a necessary trade-off, of course, but it is a possible one, especially insofar as new Canadians see the question of Indigenous reconciliation as not their problem to help solve.

4. Finally, there is Canada's success as a producer of energy. Canada is unquestionably well-endowed with energy-producing natural resources. The freshwater coverage of Quebec, Ontario, British Columbia, and Manitoba made hydroelectric power a reasonable target for long-term capital investment. The rich oil deposits of Alberta and, to a lesser but still substantial extent, Newfoundland and Labrador and Nova Scotia have enriched those provinces and indeed the whole federation. Potash extraction has, especially in recent years, enriched Saskatchewan. One part of the story here is that Canada has been lucky, in both the extent and the diversity of its natural resources. But the other part of the story is that all of these natural resources have required substantial technological and oftentimes political innovation to capitalize. Flooding huge swaths of northern Quebec was not an easy undertaking, just as tunnelling water upstream from Niagara Falls took notable engineering. Certainly, extracting oil from sand or deep offshore shelves requires some mix of entrepreneurial daring, state support, and technical acuity. So, Canada's development of energy resources has also reflected a much more impressive industrial capacity than any trope about us being hewers of wood and drawers of water would suggest.

What Canada's resource development has never shown, however, is any substantial evidence of a national project, or even sustained provincial cooperation. When the federal government has been involved, it acted either as a backstop of last resort – as in both Hibernia or the more recent purchase of the Trans-Mountain pipeline – or as a market-distorting meddler, as in the case of the oil-pricing policies culminating in the National Energy Program. When provinces have worked together on energy projects, their cooperation has often involved heavily one-sided deals, as in Churchill Falls, with the federal government clearly playing favourites. What has never been on offer is convincing evidence that the federal government can play a role that leverages the substantial energy endowments of the country to service much more than provincial interests.

This lack of evidence is doubly damning when we consider another cost imposed by our energy endowments: we have been a notable laggard on environmental sustainability. Our efforts to curb climate emissions quickly come square up against our ambitions to be an energy superpower. These competing policy goals will only make policymaking more difficult in the future.

And so here we have one of the great paradoxes of Canadian policymaking. In four key areas – federalism, Canada-U.S. relations, immigration, and natural resources – our greatest and most lasting achievements of the last fifty years have possibly set the table for policy gridlock in the next fifty.

The ongoing battle over pipelines in Canada serves as a useful example of these contending phenomena in action. What began years ago as a relatively straightforward need to get Alberta bitumen to tidewater has gradually morphed into a microcosm of the policy challenges that Canada will face in the future, incorporating all four of the perverse outcomes mentioned above: the decentralization of the federation, the overwhelming focus on the U.S. market for exports, the neglect of Indigenous interests, and the conflict between economic development and environmental action.

Over the past decade, a number of pipeline projects have been proposed and approved, only to die off thanks to court decisions, political neglect, or excessive delays driven by either grassroots activism or regulatory hoop-jumping. For example, the Northern Gateway pipeline that was supposed to bring diluted bitumen to Kitimat was approved by the federal government in 2014 (albeit with 209 conditions), but was killed a year later by Prime Minister Justin Trudeau. The Keystone XL pipeline running south to Nebraska was similarly rejected in 2015 by then-U.S. president Barack Obama, with little protest from Canada. When TransCanada cancelled its Energy East pipeline in 2017, the fact that the decision seemed to be based largely on economic grounds didn't prevent a number of Quebec politicians from celebrating it as a political victory, with Montreal mayor Denis Coderre claiming a substantial share of the credit for killing the project. Like Stephen Harper before him, Justin Trudeau has vowed that a pipeline will get built. But like Harper, Trudeau is finding that just because a project is in the national interest, it doesn't mean it will get done. If it is completed, it will likely be at massive cost to the federal treasury, with no private-sector risk sharing.

In an attempt to square their twin policy objectives of environmentalism with oil sands development, the Trudeau Liberals figured they could buy one with the other. In exchange for Alberta going along with a federal carbon tax, British Columbia would agree to the doubling of the TransMountain pipeline into Burnaby. Into this mix they added the concept of "social license," or as Trudeau famously put it, "governments can grant permits but only communities can grant permission."

Trudeau's plan to succeed where Harper had failed probably seemed like an ingenious idea at the time. But the difficulties soon mounted, beginning with the obvious problem that the very notion of social license, while undefined, seemed to offer an extralegal veto over a project to any community that happens to be in a position to do so. Even if that were resolved, it has become clear that it deliberately injected into the regulatory process a political dimension that was outside the Prime Minister's or federal government's ability to control. And thus, the seemingly clever notion of social license has turned into an n-headed monster that has sunk its claws into every possible national fracture line: Quebec versus the constitution, environmentalists versus the oil sands, Indigenous rights versus the federal government.

As Paul Wells has asked, is Canada's future a place where big things get built? Increasingly, it appears that the lessons we have learned from our past policy successes are exactly the ones that will prevent major policy transformation in the future. That's the bad news. The good news is that previous generations of Canadians have managed substantial policy transformation at critical points in the country's history. New generations can accomplish the next policy transformation, if they can recognize the need to both unlearn and learn the lessons of the past, and if they have the wisdom to know the difference.

Contributors

Aisha Ahmad is an Assistant Professor in the Department of Political Science and Director of the Islam and Global Affairs Initiative at the Munk School of Global Affairs and Public Policy at the University of Toronto.

Michelle Alexopoulos is a Professor in the Department of Economics at the University of Toronto.

Daniel Béland is a Professor in the Department of Political Science and Director of the McGill Institute for the Study of Canada at McGill University.

Sophie Borwein is a PhD Candidate in the Department of Political Science at the University of Toronto.

Jon Cohen is a Professor Emeritus in the Department of Economics at the University of Toronto.

Antje Ellermann is an Associate Professor in the Department of Political Science and Director of the Institute for European Studies at the University of British Columbia.

Kathryn Harrison is a Professor in the Department of Political Science at the University of British Columbia.

Joseph Heath is a Professor in the Department of Philosophy and the Munk School of Global Affairs and Public Policy at the University of Toronto.

Jean Leclair is a Professor in the Faculty of Law at l'Université de Montréal.

Sheryl Lightfoot is a Canada Research Chair in Global Indigenous Rights and Politics and an Associate Professor in the Department of Political Science and First Nations and Indigenous Studies Program at the University of British Columbia.

Peter John Loewen is a Professor in the Department of Political Science and the Munk School of Global Affairs and Public Policy at the University of Toronto.

Emmett Macfarlane is an Associate Professor in the Department of Political Science at the University of Waterloo.

Deborah McGregor is an Associate Professor and Canada Research Chair in Indigenous Environmental Justice at Osgoode Hall Law School and the Faculty of Environmental Studies at York University.

Kevin Milligan is a Professor in the Vancouver School of Economics at the University of British Columbia.

John Myles is a Professor Emeritus and former Canada Research Chair in the Social Foundations of Public Policy in the Department of Sociology and Senior Fellow in Public Policy at the Munk School of Global Affairs and Public Policy at the University of Toronto.

Stéphane Paquin is a Professor at l'École nationale d'administration publique.

Andrew Potter is an Associate Professor at the McGill Institute for the Study of Canada at McGill University.

Christa Scholtz is an Associate Professor in the Department of Political Science at McGill University.

Matti Siemiatycki is an Associate Professor in the Department of Geography and Planning and interim Director of the School of Cities at the University of Toronto.

Carolyn Hughes Tuohy is a Professor Emeritus in the Department of Political Science and Founding Fellow in Public Policy at the Munk School of Global Affairs and Public Policy at the University of Toronto.

Michael Valpy is a journalist and Senior Fellow in Public Policy at the Munk School of Global Affairs and Public Policy at the University of Toronto.

Jeremy Webber is a Professor and former Canada Research Chair in the Faculty of Law at the University of Victoria.

Jennifer Winter is an Assistant Professor in the Department of Economics and Scientific Director of Energy and Environmental Policy at the School of Public Policy at the University of Calgary.

Lightning Source UK Ltd.
Milton Keynes UK
UKHW010726170419
341161UK00001B/82/P